THOM FILICIA
STYLE

THOM FILICIA
STYLE

Inspired Ideas for Creating Rooms You'll Love

ATRIA BOOKS
New York London Toronto Sydney

You know who you are...

Thank you to Kathleen Renda for her incredible writing, dedication, and talent. It's not easy to go into my head and come out alive, let alone with fabulous prose. Tremendous thanks also to Judith Nasatir, whose skill in articulating my vision is unsurpassed.

Special thanks to Atria/Simon & Schuster, including our extraordinary editor, Peter Borland.

I want to gratefully acknowledge the incomparable art director Doug Turshen for his talent (and patience!), Steve Turner for his brilliant graphic design, and especially, especially Chardonnay Pickard, without whose work this book wouldn't have been completed (sort of) on time.

Major thanks to genius photographers Eric Piasecki, Toshiaki Nozawa-san, Jonny Valiant, Antonis Achilleos, Thomas Loof, Barbel Miebach, William Waldron, Michael Reynolds, Brad Stein, Paul Costello, Jeff Clark, François Halard, Jason Schmidt, Dale Berman, Jeffrey Thurnher, Brooke Jacobs, Howard Wise, and William Abranowicz.

Sincerest gratitude to the many publications and editors that have supported me, particularly: *Elle Decor* and Peggy Russell; *O at Home* and Sarah Gray Miller and Natalie Warady; *House & Garden* and Dominique Browning and Mayer Rus; *Interior Design* and Cindy Allen; *Domino* and Deborah Needleman, Sara Ruffin Costello and Dara Caponigro; the *Today* show; *House Beautiful* and Stephen Drucker and Newell Turner; *New York* and Wendy Goodman; *Teen Vogue* and Amy Astley; *InStyle* and Charla Lawhorn; *Blackbook* and Steve Garbarino; *Hamptons* and Cristina Greeven-Cuomo and Jill Sieracki; *The Atlanta Peach* and Elizabeth Schulte Roth; *The Advocate*; *Boutique Design* and Michael Schneider; *Array* and Paul Millman; *USA Today*; and the *New York Times*. And every other magazine we've ever worked with—thanks!

Thank you to all of the television shows and producers who believed in me, especially *The Oprah Winfrey Show*, *The Ellen DeGeneres Show*, *The Tonight Show with Jay Leno*, *Late Night with Conan O'Brien*, the *Today* show, *The Early Show*, *The View*, *Queer Eye for the Straight Guy*, and every show I've appeared on.

Warmest thanks to Mr. Hadley, the dean of interior design, for your generosity, guidance and unparalleled knowledge.

Thank you to everyone I grew up with in Syracuse, New York, who made me the person I am today. Many thanks to the Everson Museum and Sandra Trop, the Century Club, Mary Ellen Anders, Gary Pickard, and all my professors at Syracuse University.

I am so grateful to my public relations firm, The Brooks Group and Rebecca Brooks, Erika Martineau, Nicky Turlington, and David Hawkins.

Thanks to my incredible literary agents, David Vigliano and Michael Harriot, who made this book happen.

Thanks to the William Morris Agency, particularly Adam Sher and Steven Grossman for their steadfast guidance. Gratitude to Keith Granet for his know-how, and to Bob Myman and Jennifer Grega for their expert legal advice.

Deepest gratitude to Fred Bernstein and his genius idea that I be photographed in front of Bryan Nash Gill's sycamore screen.

Thanks to my entire family, especially my dad, Thomas, my stepmom, Sue, my brothers James and his wife, Theresa, and Jules and his wife, Leslie, and all my amazing nieces and nephews. I love you all very, very much.

Thank you to everyone at Style Network for their support in making *Dress My Nest* a reality.

My heartfelt gratitude to the top-notch production company PB&J, especially Patty Ivans and Julie Pizzi, and Jeff Kuntz and Damon Zwicker for their talent as directors. And a major shout-out to Mike Carney and Allison Carroll, my incomparable production team, who work harder than anybody.

Of course thanks to my amazing partner, Greg Calejo, who has not only put up with me for more years than I wish to mention, but has supported me both professionally and personally. Plus our dogs, Paco and Foxy.

Thanks to all the vendors, retailers, contractors, and artists that have made this book a success. Your products, artwork, and services are the best, and I thank you for sharing them. Particular thanks to Larsen/Cowtan & Tout (and the amazing Key Hall and Miry Park)—your slate wall covering is so gorgeous I couldn't help but plaster it on the cover! Huge, huge thanks to Corvin Mattei and his superb renderings. Plus Kravet, Aero, FJ Hakimian, Calypso, John Derian, Brentano's Framing, Bark Frameworks, JCPenney, Karastan, Crate & Barrel, Serta, West Elm, Room & Board, Benjamin Moore, Mecox Gardens, Jonathan Wigmore, Museum Editions, Gavin Ziegler, Gregory Miller, Steve Fanukah, Mark Nichols, Lulu DK, and Studio Printworks. Special thanks to Ethan Allen and their amazing support of the family room makeover. A hearty thanks to the courageous Sherri Burmester and the entire Burmester clan, who allowed us to make over her bedroom in conjunction with Serta and Susan G. Komen. And of course the Ethridges, the fantastic family in Massachusetts who won our nationwide makeover contest.

Major thanks to the entire team at W Hotel, especially Ross Klein, whose support, vision, and friendship have been invaluable to me over the years.

I am eternally indebted to the incredible team at Thom Filicia Inc., without whose support, dedication, and hard work I could never have finished this book, let alone our multitude of projects.

And Marc Szafran. I really don't know how to put this into words. This book would never, ever have happened without you. Honestly, you were the driving force behind the entire project, keeping me in line and on schedule. You were determined, committed, passionate, focused, dogged, accommodating, encouraging, enthusiastic, and unwavering. And you made me actually enjoy the process. You're the reason we were able to accomplish this, and none of it would have happened without you.

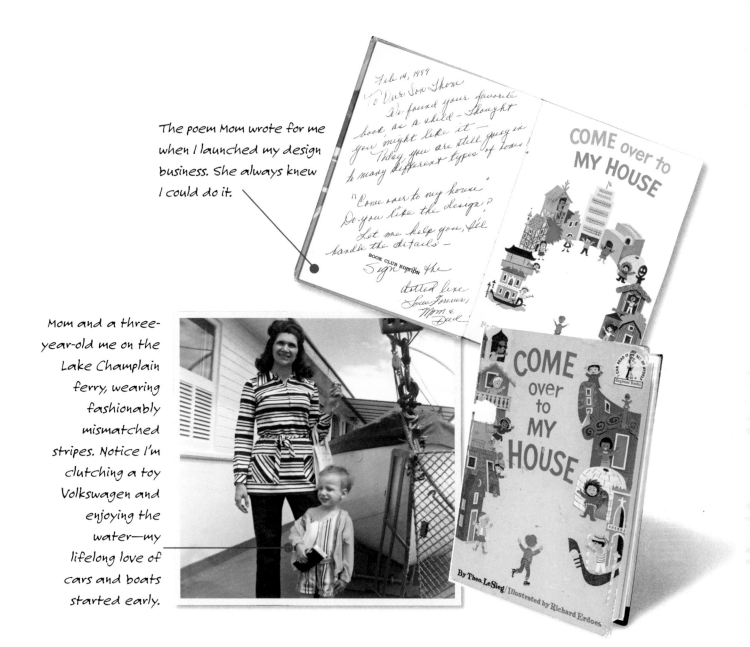

The poem Mom wrote for me when I launched my design business. She always knew I could do it.

Feb 14, 1999
To Our Son Thom
We found your favorite book as a child — Thought you might like it —
Today, you are still going to many different types of homes!

"Come over to my house" Do you like the design?
Let me help you, I'll handle the details —
Sign on the
dotted line
Love Forever,
Mom & Dad

Mom and a three-year-old me on the Lake Champlain ferry, wearing fashionably mismatched stripes. Notice I'm clutching a toy Volkswagen and enjoying the water—my lifelong love of cars and boats started early.

Janet Katherine Filicia (1939–2002)

This book is dedicated to my one-of-a-kind mom. She was creative and nurturing and as much fun as she was fabulous. I'm indebted to her for my sense of style and humor, and my love of people, places, and things.

Mom always read me my favorite bedtime story, Dr. Seuss's *Come Over to My House*. It's about a little boy who travels from house to house around the world, meeting kids and learning about their cultures and customs. The story—about visiting homes and understanding the people in them—is essentially my career today. Mom made that connection. And when I launched my design business, she gave me the book inscribed with a poem she wrote. I read that poem aloud at her funeral.

We lost Mom to breast cancer. She's not here to celebrate the publication of this book, but in a way she will be: proceeds from the sale of this book will be donated to support breast cancer research and awareness. I miss you, Mom.

**Forever, love
Thom**

Contents

PART I: PROCESS

How do you transform your personal aesthetic into an inviting interior? Follow my ten fail-safe tips, culled from fifteen-plus years in the design business. Covering everything from layout to lighting to color to artfully mixing clashing patterns, consider them your starter kit for style.

Rooms have feelings, too. They can be organic, refined, sexy, pure, warm, balanced, fun, inviting, and exotic (plus one surprise). Strategies for achieving the best moods for your space.

Combine my ten tips with my ten favorite moods and you'll have rooms that are far more than the sum of their parts. A brief primer on how to make all-important connections that lead to happy habitation.

PART II: CASE STUDIES

A hip young couple's urban loft becomes family friendly thanks to smart space usage and sturdy-but-stylish furnishings that can stand up to the demands of daily living.

The master bedroom of a courageous breast cancer survivor gets a chic tweak and transforms into both a cozy family hangout spot and a private sanctuary for Mom.

On *Dress My Nest*, fashion and personal items are jumping-off points for determining decor. This insider's look into one of my favorite episodes shows what happens when a celebrity couple struggle to merge their decors after saying "I do."

Today's eco-living is as stylish as it is sustainable. Highlights from my handiwork at Riverhouse, Manhattan's most earth-friendly residential building.

Meet the Ethridge clan, winners of my first-ever family-room makeover contest, and learn how a great room can become amazing.

FOREWORD

STYLE as presented by Thom Filicia resembles more a gleaming locomotive racing cross-country than it does a soft but determined breeze.

Thom's well-mannered personal style embraces with clarity a fair measure of a sometimes wicked wit. Nonsense is out of the question, but an exemplary degree of knowledgeable and cultivated taste forms the mantra upon which his work is founded.

I remember with nostalgia and admiration the enthusiastic and career-driven young man, recently graduated from college, who joined the ranks of the design team at Parish-Hadley, Inc. That was just the beginning!

Those who may not know in detail of Filicia's accomplishments will, no doubt, glean that information and more in the pages of this fantastic guide book. I refer to the content in this manner because the book has been brilliantly divided into sections, all of which exude imagination, super style, and that sometimes elusive quality of paramount personal taste.

Go to it! Have fun! You're on your own—but remember—Thom Filicia is always there!

—Albert Hadley, May 2008

MY MENTOR, MR. HADLEY

I'm incredibly lucky that Albert Hadley was my first boss when I was just starting out in the business sixteen years ago. As one of the leading designers of the last century (his clients included Jackie O, Babe Paley, and the Astor and Getty families), he helped shape my aesthetic and showed me that rooms could be as chic as they are comfortable. And every time I see this photo of a Manhattan showhouse I created with classic, refined, inventive, fun, and serious elements, I'm reminded of how much Albert influenced me—and, I'm hoping, you.

INTRODUCTION

I bet I can guess what you're thinking right about now. Probably something like: Isn't this that interior design guy from television? Why did he write a book? Well, it's true—I was part of the Fab Five on *Queer Eye* and now I'm doing *Dress My Nest,* and this is my first solo book—but that's only part of the story. Because the Thom Filicia you see on television revamping spaces on a budget is just me moonlighting. In my offscreen day job, the one I've been working at since I graduated from Syracuse University with a degree in interior design, I create high-end interiors for high-profile clients (think Jennifer Lopez and the W Hotels chain). It all happens with the help of fifteen overcaffeinated, amazing, and totally dedicated staffers at my namesake firm, Thom Filicia Inc., otherwise known as "TFI." I opened TFI's doors in Manhattan back in 1998, and now we're global, designing residential and commercial projects from the Hamptons to Japan. Combined with my television shows, it makes for an exciting, crazy-busy work life. One day I might be creating a luxe Park Avenue apartment with all its accoutrements for a private client. The next, I'm in a modest Los Angeles abode installing a living room while the cameras are rolling—and I have to say, I can't imagine doing one without the other.

While I love designing high-end projects, I get equal satisfaction in doing television. I can reach an incredibly diverse audience, and the constraints on the clock and costs force me to be hypercreative. But television decorating has one drawback: unlike the individualized attention I can give to my clients, there's only a finite amount of design info viewers can absorb from a program. The next best solution to cloning myself: a book that deconstructs step-by-step what I do, with smart strategies and try-this-at-home ideas. And just as I do on television and for my private clients, my hope is that this book will give you the confidence to express your personality through your home—a home that, if you follow my no-nonsense, straightforward advice and trust yourself, will always be fun, classic with a modern twist, fresh and bold . . . and uniquely yours.

So consider the following pages as your all-access pass to what goes on inside my brain (kinda scary), at my firm, and behind the cameras. There's the My Philosophy section, which outlines my beliefs that great design is achievable by anyone and that the best interiors reflect the character and spirit of the person who lives there. In the Process chapters, I divulge my hush-hush, insider secrets and the ten moods I try to evoke in everything I design. And in the Case Studies, you get to witness me in action, applying my philosophy and process to actual, real-world homes, so you can learn to do the same creative problem-solving successfully on your own.

It's *Thom Filicia Style.* The best of both of my worlds. For you. Now let's get started . . .

xoxo
Thom

Treat this book as a how-to guide for self-expression with style. It will teach you to turn your passions and priorities into chic interiors that are distinctive, inviting, and totally you. (And check out the secret password on the back flap for exclusive access to my tie-in Web site.)

SHOW AND TELL

This photo, snapped during a rare nanosecond of downtime during the filming of *Dress My Nest*, really captures what this book is all about. I'm about to take you behind the scenes of my design process, explaining my tools, techniques, and tricks, and empowering you to create rooms that embrace and accommodate who you really are.

First Things First

My name is Thomas Leonard Filicia Junior, but you can call me Thom. A big thanks for buying my book. I can hardly spell, so this wasn't an easy task. I think the only thing more stressed out than me during this whole writing shenanigan was the spell check on my computer. Which may have exploded or caught on

70s: The Formative Years

Chez Filicia in the historic neighborhood of Sedgwick Farm. Listen closely and you can hear me getting yelled at.

Mom working the Jackie O look. Not sure why I'm in white—I was never an angel.

I come into the world in 1969 in upstate New York, the third son of Thomas Senior and Janet Filicia. Our house is always high-decibel and raucous, what with three boys, a yapping poodle, and parents trying to contain all the kid-caused commotions (OK, we're maniacs). My fun-loving mom is a creative dynamo with a flair for the dramatic—she once wore her full-length mink coat on my fourth-grade field trip to the Beaver Lake Nature Center. As a child, I dream of becoming an architect. At nine, I land my first commission: a slope-roof fort that I build with my dad. I'm a happy kid, except when I hide in the bathroom, convinced my brothers, Jim and Jules, are going to suffocate me. Which is pretty much all the time.

80s: The Social Years

Flock of Seagulls meets the Preppy Handbook. Note the pink-and-green tie and Polo button-down oxford. Stylin'!

Interior shots of our house taken for my high school photography class. I thought these black-and-white prints looked "arty."

High school for me is advanced art, architectural drafting, ski club, and throwing parties every time my parents leave the house for more than two hours. Mom lets us decorate our bedrooms however we want, so I swap my tweenager orange shag carpeting and beanbag chairs for grown-up hardwood floors and light gray walls. Summers I spend at Camp Tousey and not studying for the SATs. I love camp so much that I go back as a counselor-in-training and then as a counselor, where I teach water-skiing, sailing, and swimming, and work as a lifeguard. The SATs don't go so well.

fire—I'm not sure, but there was definitely a burning smell. Maybe it's better if you just look at the photos. They chart my upbringing and major life milestones, detail how I got where I am today, and explain why I'm like this (although there probably isn't a good explanation). And no, none of the snapshots were retouched. If they were, I'd look a lot better.

Early 90s: The *Really* Social Years

In Santorini, Greece, repurposing a hotel bedspread as party attire.

My alma mater, Syracuse. Amazingly, they now let me guest-lecture.

My college yearbook photo. Love the blunt bob, turquoise blazer, fraternity pin, and bow tie. I must have been hungover to put this look together.

College. It's a miracle I make it in, make it through, and make it out with a degree (on the five-year plan). I'm enrolled in Syracuse University studying interior design (calculus—or failing calculus—ended my architecture dreams), and I'm social chair at my fraternity, which is similar to throwing parties in high school but with a budget. I'm still thankful that no one drowned in the aboveground, indoor pool I installed in my fraternity house basement for our Fiji Island bash—in January. During summers, I work in Nantucket, island-hop on the cheap in Greece, and luckily land an internship at Parish-Hadley in Manhattan, one of the country's most venerable design firms.

Mid-to-late 90s: The Early Professional Years

Parish-Hadley. Hallelujah! Thom's employable and paying taxes. Who would have thought?

My first Manhattan apartment. I found the blue vinyl chair—which I still have—in the building's trash room.

Postcollege, I finagle my internship at Parish-Hadley into a full-time assistant job there. I hunt down fabrics, spend hours drawing and redrawing floor plans, and eagerly accept even the most menial tasks and love every minute of it. Money is tight, so I bunk with two friends in the then-unfashionable neighborhood of Murray Hill. We're three young professionals excited about living our "fabulous" urban lives on entry-level paychecks. Our apartment is decorated with family hand-me-downs, flea market finds, and other people's trash—hey, it's our treasure. These are the struggling years of three-to-a-bedroom summer-house shares, twelve-hour workdays, and learning everything I can about design.

Late 90s: Who's the Boss

When your mom says it's a bad photo, you know it's a bad photo.

Following Parish-Hadley, I have some incredible years at the offices of Robert Metzger Interiors and Jeffrey Bilhuber Incorporated. I finally decide to strike out on my own, in 1998, and with trepidation and excitement, I open Thom Filicia Inc. To my utter amazement, *W* magazine names me as an up-and-coming designer. Thrilled, nervous, and unaccustomed to press coverage, I pose for the article in a professorial turtleneck sweater, looking like a deer caught in the headlights. Not long after, *House & Garden* does eight pages on an apartment I designed in South Beach. To no one's surprise, my photo doesn't appear with the story.

The 2000s: Picture Perfect

If Queer Eye didn't out me, this certainly did.

With a lot of diligence, hustle, and perseverance on my part, the business begins to really take off. The size of both my staff and my projects increases, and the *New York Times* and more shelter magazines feature my work. *House Beautiful* includes me in its roundup of the country's Top 100 designers, and *House & Garden* later puts me on its list of the Top 50 Tastemakers. I'm ecstatic and honored, especially when the custom furniture I designed is included in the photos. I pose for the pics dressed as a modern-day Rudolph Valentino, complete with velvet slippers, white linen pants, and slicked-back hairdo. My brothers still tease me about it.

The Mid-2000s: Turning the Page

The "hip and classic" cover line sums it all up. I just hope it's true.

These years are mostly a caffeinated blur. I'm taping *Queer Eye*, giving lectures, doing media appearances, being profiled in magazines and newspapers—plus the business is going full throttle, with both residential and commercial clients. Thank God for my supersupportive staff and iced skim lattes with Splenda. The two biggest pinch-me moments: the estate I revamp for Jennifer Lopez and Marc Anthony appears on the inaugural issue of *Vogue Living*; less than a year later, *Elle Decor* runs a feature on my SoHo apartment.

2007: Fashion Forward

Finally, a not-too-shabby photo.

My first interior design show, *Dress My Nest*, premieres on the Style Network. I'm working with the ladies and loving it, but headlining my own show is about a million times more complicated than I anticipated. After filming more than a hundred episodes as part of an ensemble cast on *Queer Eye*, doing a solo series is like being an unsure undergrad all over again. I gain the freshman fifteen (pounds, that is). My fans follow me to the new series, and the show's a success. We're renewed! I go on a diet.

2003: Prime Time

I guess I was prepared if it was gonna start raining men.

I audition for a new Bravo reality series and somehow get picked to participate. It doesn't really hit me until the show's about to air that it's titled *Queer Eye for the Straight Guy*. When the program premieres, it's all-out craziness: there's a billboard of the Fab Five in Times Square, we land on the cover of *Entertainment Weekly*, and the show becomes a critical and commercial success almost overnight. And I couldn't have been more shocked or unprepared. Especially when I find myself standing on stage accepting an Emmy for Outstanding Reality Program. Who would have thought—an interior designer with an Emmy?

2004: Show and Tell

Sometimes you have to pinch yourself to make sure you aren't dreaming.

All of a sudden, the Fab Five are appearing on talk shows and live morning programs (no pressure!), from *Regis and Kelly* to *The View* to the *Today* show to *Oprah* to *Ellen* to *Conan* to Barbara Walter's most-fascinating-people special. Thankfully I don't get tongue-tied, bleeped, or booted off, since my excitement usually cancels out my nervousness. Except that one time before a live taping of *The Tonight Show with Jay Leno*. I'm so terrified that I drink the entire contents of the green room's bar cart. The fab five of us have tons of fun, and I'm fortunate to get invited back.

2008: The Life Aquatic

Don't drink and drive.

With fond, semifalse childhood memories of all the fun afternoons my family spent boating on the Finger Lakes near Syracuse, I buy a ramshackle house on a lake in upstate New York (which *Domino* features in their summer issue). It's a never-ending renovation project but a great getaway from the Manhattan pressure cooker. Greg and I road-trip there almost every weekend, bringing along the dogs, Paco and Foxy, and as many friends as I can convince that I'm actually a skilled water-skier—and skipper. All the boat propellers I damage are displayed on the coffee table like artwork. It's an ever-growing collection.

2008: A Novel Idea

Yes, I'm holding a plastic cardinal. Guess who's the birdbrain . . .

Thom Filicia Style, my first how-to guide, hits store shelves nationwide. It's a way for people to bring me home in convenient (and less annoying) book form.

MY PHILOSOPHY

I'm a democratic design snob. I see it as my mission to help stamp out boring, unimaginative interiors. But I also love people, having fun, and what I do for a living. I think a fabulously styled place is achievable by everyone, and with the crazy abundance of decorating resources and info available today via the Internet and television shows (some better than others—see *Dress My Nest* on the Style Network, and you be the judge), there's almost no reason to have bad taste, so listen up.

It doesn't matter if your place is a mountain hideaway, a houseboat, a 10,000-square-foot beach bungalow for two, a city loft, or a split-level in suburbia. Everyone everywhere can love where they live—and should—and it's doable no matter the size of their space or budget, or their level of decorating confidence. Because pulling off dynamic, distinctive interiors you're happy to come home to isn't always about breaking the bank or having a decorator on speed dial (even if it's me). It's really about creating rooms that are true to you, that reflect your personality and who you really are. And who knows you better than you? You have total access to all your unique likes and dislikes, what makes you happiest, and what's most meaningful to you. I'm just here to help you figure that out and to provide the guidance and know-how to translate who you are into how you live—only better. Think of me as your decorating wingman, someone who'll advise, support, inspire (and occasionally browbeat) you, so you don't have to white-knuckle it alone. And by the end of the book, you'll be sufficiently prepped to go at it solo. With style—your style.

PIED-DE-THOM

Manhattan is famous for historical apartments with period details. Mine isn't one of them. Built in 2004, it was bland and featureless, so I tweaked the space to give it some much-needed character (you'll be seeing photos of all my handiwork on the next ten pages). In the living room, *right*, that meant staining the standard-issue cherry floors a rich ebony, raising the anemic baseboards to a heftier twelve inches, and hanging textured wallpaper. This created a clean-lined backdrop for the apartment's style, which is part urban, part sophisticated, and part modern—and totally me.

This custom console is a high-flying homage to an eagle that nests near my lake house in upstate New York—and to Georgian-style avian motifs.

THROUGH THE LOOKING GLASS

What my newly built SoHo apartment lacked in millwork and graciousness, it more than made up for in location. Built on the western edge of Manhattan just a few blocks from the Hudson River, it has sweeping views of the New Jersey coastline and oceangoing ships and sailboats. To take full advantage of the always-changing vistas outside my window, I made a gutsy decision to replace the wall separating the living room and the bedroom with industrial safety glass. It was a dramatic change that totally opened up the interior, giving me amazing sight lines from every room and creating a loftlike sense of free-flowing spaciousness. The glass, embedded with crosshatched wires, is also a nod to the neighborhood's manufacturing past and helps establish the apartment's signature look of downtown-gritty-meets-uptown-refined. Also helping to bring all the decade- and style-spanning pieces together: a watery palette of misty grays and blues and greens that echoes the colors outside.

Stretching nine feet and based on a traditional English Chesterfield style, the nap-worthy Saratoga sofa I designed is updated with square arms and simple lines and visually anchors the room.

I love the curvaceousness of these nineteenth-century Italian chairs. Newly upholstered in linen, they look crisp and fresh.

That's my dog Paco, snoozing as usual.

When *Queer Eye* premiered in 2003, with me as one of the Fab Five, it was groundbreaking television in more ways than one. There was the obvious (hello, a quintet of openly out guys), but it was also one of the first-ever shows to empower the homeowners, transforming them into active, hands-on participants in the design overhaul. This wasn't your standard makeover show. Instead, it was a make-better show. It identified the person's best, sometimes hidden, attributes and elevated them to a more stylish level—like the theme song's "all things just keep getting better" lyrics suggested. Until then, the trend was for decorating shows to manufacture tension by cutting the homeowners out of the process until the finale. A room decorated with zero input from the person who will actually live there might have been dramatic and humorous, but it wasn't exactly inspired design. What made *Queer Eye* so innovative—and so popular—was that it proved that even the style-challenged could get enthused about interior design and be a part of the process. During every episode, each guy quickly learned the basics of creating personalized interiors and discovered the highly opinionated decorator within. The subtext was that you, the viewer, could do the same in your place—but do it even better, because you weren't as design-impaired. In every episode, I identified an object that was important to the guy—and it wasn't easy, because sometimes I found it in a pizza box under the sofa—which defined his personality or his outlook on life, and then utilized it as a springboard to influence the entire look of our design. With some insightful questioning and thoughtful shopping, he realized that yes, he did have taste, and yes, he could learn to create an interior that was as individualized as it was amazing—a space that reflected the best of him and not just my arbitrary choices or the latest trends in home decor. The formula proved so winning that it eventually evolved into my hit series *Dress My* (continues on pg. 24)

EAT IN OR TAKE OUT

Because I entertain frequently and have an open floor plan, my decor needs to be flexible and multitasking, and that's especially true in my dining area. Less a place to eat and more an extension of the living room, it's a home office when I'm working late on renderings, a serve-yourself buffet during parties, and a mini gallery for artwork. For tackling all of that, I chose a substantial circular table with lots of surface area and enough heft to balance both a sizable painting and an organic wood sculpture.

Proof that sometimes more is more: this huge waterscape by artist and surfer Alex Weinstein, complements the apartment's maritime palette.

Lightweight and easy to move, these grab-and-go French chairs provide extra seating wherever it's needed. The rope webbing is both textural and a nod to the apartment's nautical influences.

In my apartment, livability and luxe aren't mutually exclusive. The suede-upholstered sofa is a favorite snoozing spot for my dog Paco—and I wouldn't have it any other way.

SWATCH AND LEARN

The locale and the light were the inspiration for my apartment's color and texture palette. Outside my west-facing windows are the Hudson River and the urban New Jersey skyline, and I brought indoors those same hues—the grayish-blue water and the deep, rusted reds of the sun setting over glass and steel and concrete. The mix is masculine, modern, sexy, and rich, and the fabrics and materials reinforce that vibe. I used a geek-chic perforated suede with a pattern that evokes electrical circuitry, classic gray-veined marble, elegant black cashmere, sage lambskin leather, industrial safety glass, and a silk velvet pillow printed with stylized leaves. Together, they reflect all the complexities and contradictions of the city—and the apartment—I've made my home.

Yes, the antique rug's a little tattered, and that's what makes it perfect—it immediately telegraphs to guests that this is a laid-back apartment where you can kick back, relax, and not worry about using a coaster.

Chairs can substitute for entryway tables when space is at a premium. I stack mine with oversized books—then top with an orchid to prevent it from becoming a way station for clutter.

Nest, in which I help gals who rock their wardrobes bring that same creativity and confidence to their interiors. Focusing on fashion and their favorite possessions is how I dialogue with them. I ask them to pick out their three favorite fashion items and their three favorite personal items, and this gives me an understanding of their hopefully fabulous style. These selections, because of everything they represent and how they make her feel, become the jumping-off point for the gal's new space. The result is a home that not only looks gorgeous but also functions fabulously, has heart and soul, and tells her story.

While decorating based on what's significant to a homeowner generated a lot of enthusiastic buzz from viewers and critics, it wasn't a new approach for me. It's always been my guiding philosophy, from the moment I opened my firm, Thom Filicia Inc., in 1998. I can't pinpoint exactly why I do this—maybe in another life I was a psychotherapist or a private detective, or maybe I just like people more than the next guy—but from my first meeting with my clients I want to find out what makes them tick. We sit down, we chat, we travel, we have a cocktail (or five), and I discover who they are and what they're about. I'm interested in what vehicle they drive, where they vacation and their all-time favorite getaway, their music, their relationship with their family and friends, how they entertain, what kind of pets they own, the works. Discovering that a client splurges on high-end designer shoes but economizes on technology—or vice versa—is very telling. So is the food (or lack thereof) in their refrigerator, the drink they always order at a bar, and the items already in their homes. Using that info, I get a complete sense of the person, and that ultimately directs how their place should look, feel, and function—because

FLIGHTS OF FANCY

As the most intimate, private spot in the apartment, my bedroom showcases the pieces that reveal who I am and what I really value. This pair of sterling silver heirloom peacocks, *above,* once belonged to my grandmother and were passed down to me from my mom—think it's any coincidence that they're the birds with the most flamboyant plumage? A charcoal sketch of my rescued dog Paco, *right,* was affordable compared to my other gallery-purchased artwork, but it gets pride of place beside my desk.

Organic and slightly sinister, this edgy skeleton-shaped aluminum desk chair shakes up a classic four-poster bed and traditional Chinese console table.

the greatest inspiration for an interior is the person or people who are going to live there, and my goal is to connect them with a great-looking design that's appropriate to their lifestyle, interests, and points of view.

All of my finished projects are as different as my clients. But there is some commonality—it's not like anything goes. Although my designs start and end with what's important to the client, in between they're shaped by my aesthetic of classic simplicity with modern flair and my long-held belief that great design can be had at every price point. I love strong, unfussy lines, rich texture, and forever-classic hues punctuated by bold pops of color. I'm not afraid to mix mass-market with custom-made, affordable with ultraexpensive, high-end with low. The resulting look is simultaneously accessible, sophisticated, comfortable, fun, and rooted in tradition but still up-to-the-minute—and since I'm along for the ride, totally achievable. By the end of this book, you'll have a Mini-Me in your head to help you recognize what's chic, what's not, and what's you.

To pull this off, I'm opening my design portfolio to show you how I helped clients achieve their own state of superpersonal chic. In fact, I've started with one of my toughest cases—me. I'm a quirky Manhattan bachelor with an outlandish sense of humor who rarely cooks but loves to entertain, constantly throws cocktail parties, lets his dog snooze on all the furniture, has been called a workaholic, and insists on displaying his Emmy award as his powder-room toilet-paper holder. That's a lot to design around, but as the last ten pages featuring my apartment show, still absolutely doable. As a get-to-know-you intro to my signature style, I hope this section entices you to join in the design adventure that unfolds over the next two hundred pages.

KITCHEN AID

Melding different textures and sensibilities, the kitchen is compact but makes a big style statement. The overall look is sleek and sophisticated, because it needed to transition seamlessly into the living room. For continuity, the upper cabinets were painted the same charcoal-gray as the baseboards and the trim, and the almost-black slate tiles underfoot have a similar hue to the ebonized wood floors used in other rooms. Refined pendant lights and a pair of rope-wrapped stools adds to the unkitcheny feel.

A quick trick to add insta-chic to any kitchen? Treat the countertop as a gallery for displaying artwork—just avoid culinary clichés like photos of foods or paintings of forks.

For a unique look, I painted the existing cabinetry an exotic Chinese red and replaced the hardware with the same stainless-steel flush-mounted latches used on boats.

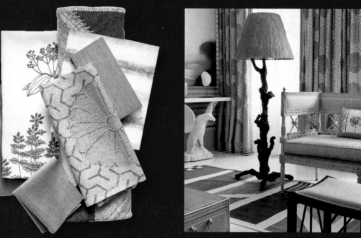

Part I PROCESS

What I do seems to baffle people. How is it I can go into a room and instantly know what colors to paint the walls, where to position the sofa, and how to artfully balance a disparate mix of styles, price points, and eras? Well, I have a confession to make: decorating isn't as inscrutable or mysterious as it comes across. It might seem intuitive and out of reach, but there are fundamentals I adhere to and a method I follow that anyone can reproduce. In this section, I'm breaking down that process into easily understandable steps, so you can learn to design stylish, comfortable interiors on your own. As I mention in the Philosophy section, your surroundings should be an extension of who you are, reflecting the ongoing narrative of your life. Making those rooms chic starts with focusing on how you want the space not to look but to *feel*. I'm also distilling my fifteen-plus years of design experience into ten simple, surprising tips— let's call them Thom's Ten Tips—for inspired decorating, accompanied by dozens of examples on how to apply each to your surroundings. To help you understand how important mood is to the success of a design, I'm identifying my nine go-to favorites (plus one wild card) that form the basis of my interiors and pointing you toward the materials, colors, and furnishings that foster those feelings. Then I give you a quick primer on how to pull it all together. That's not so hard, is it?

TIP #1: Lay out a plan

Every successful room starts with a successful floor plan. Furniture that's arranged effectively can maximize square footage, downplay architectural drawbacks, and easily accommodate a variety of activities. Configure a room so that the layout feels organic to the space, and it instantly seems more inviting. This kind of smart layout allows for smooth traffic flow and multitasking efficiency—and will look amazing. It can visually improve a room's proportions, making small areas seem larger and cavernous spaces seem cozier.

Poorly planned rooms are the number one decorating problem I encounter, whether I'm redoing a SoHo loft or a Hamptons beach house or a starter apartment on *Dress My Nest*. The second I walk into a client's space I'm mentally moving the furniture around, auditioning different setups that are more appealing and more appropriate to their needs and day-to-day activities. Like a bed that's facing directly toward the closet and the bathroom, which offers less-than-attractive sight lines to clothes and a toilet—not what I would call a room with a view. No one wants to see that every morning and every night, so I'd reposition the bed to look out the window and the wider, toiletless world beyond—even if that means floating the bed in the middle of the room. Or I'll take an underused area at the edge of a family room, where there's maybe just a lone, forlorn floor lamp, and add some friendly pieces, like a small game table and a pair of comfy armchairs, and transform the spot into a casual hangout zone.

To make the most of your space, don't default to the most obvious floor plan (although that sometimes works, too). Start with the largest anchor pieces and then get creative. Try trial and error and be willing to experiment. A room's floor plan should evolve over time and acclimate to changing situations. Keep the furniture arrangement loose and open to possibilities. Deviate from the expected, and your room will gain livability, chicness, and no shortage of comfort.

BEFORE

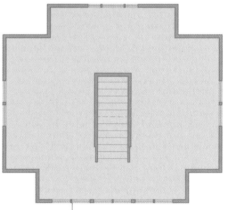

SPACE CRAFT

Taking this unfinished, second-story Hamptons guesthouse from gutted to gorgeous required some clever space-enhancing tricks. The biggest design challenges: finding a nonclaustrophobic way to delineate the open-plan room into separate sleeping and living sections and working around a stairwell smack in the middle of the space.

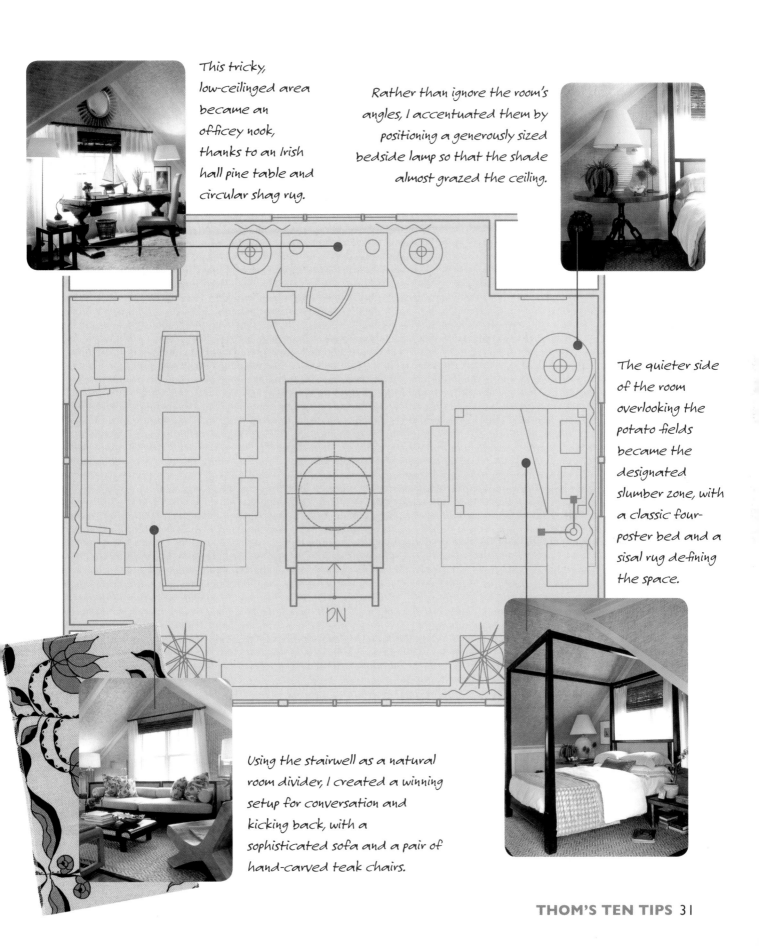

This tricky, low-ceilinged area became an officey nook, thanks to an Irish hall pine table and circular shag rug.

Rather than ignore the room's angles, I accentuated them by positioning a generously sized bedside lamp so that the shade almost grazed the ceiling.

The quieter side of the room overlooking the potato fields became the designated slumber zone, with a classic four-poster bed and a sisal rug defining the space.

Using the stairwell as a natural room divider, I created a winning setup for conversation and kicking back, with a sophisticated sofa and a pair of hand-carved teak chairs.

DN

Let the room's proportions and architecture —here, a low-sloping ceiling and short side walls—help guide the floor plan and the furniture choices.

Four-poster beds create the feeling of a room-within-a-room, important in a large space or a loftlike interior lacking walls and doors.

ALL TOGETHER NOW

Recurring textures and a beachy palette that's more stylish than salty unify the free-flowing, 500-square-foot space. Swathing the entire room, including the ceiling, with woven grasscloth backed by charcoal-paper makes the space feel less flat and gives it substance. Identical black-bordered, natural-fiber rugs in the sleep and lounge areas carry the effect onto the floors.

A large, overstuffed sofa would have felt too bulky and would have overwhelmed the room. A better choice: a lean and classic sofa with a precise silhouette.

Balinese hand-carved teak chairs lend an exotic hint of faraway shores and read like sculpture.

It was the greatest of all great rooms, with 29-foot vaulted ceilings and a walk-in fireplace.

To raise funds for charity, organizations frequently stage designer showhouses, in which they invite the likes of me to redecorate the rooms before throwing open the doors to the public for tours and lectures. I've done a number of these, but one of the most exciting was at the Greystone Estate in Beverly Hills. Built in 1928 by the son of an oil baron, Greystone is a 55-room, Tudor-style mansion with an astonishing 46,000 square feet sprawled over 16 acres of coveted California real estate. The formal living room I was given to decorate was one of the home's most spectacular spaces, with coffered, 29-foot cathedral ceilings, 19-foot leaded glass windows, massive scrolled archways, a walk-in fireplace, and hand-carved mahogany paneling. While few of us live in places with this kind of epic grandeur, that doesn't mean there aren't takeaway lessons here for your interiors. Like dealing with those castlelike proportions. One of my priorities was to bring the grandness down to a human scale and create a layout that felt intimate. But I also wanted to update the room in a way that felt respectful to the architecture and to the mansion's storied past,

BEFORE

and in sync with the way people really live today. A room that would be approachable and comfortable, sophisticated and refined, mindful of history and still forward-looking—and that's exactly what I achieved. Showhouses are amazing idea labs, where you can audition styles and solutions that are adaptable to any home and budget—and where you can pick up tons of decorating dos (and don'ts). Greystone is a perfect example of how a high-design room can feel totally down-to-earth. Really.

DIVIDE AND CONQUER

The strategy for a room this huge—at one end there's an enormous, double-height bay window, at the other end is an arched entranceway, and in between there's a lot of empty space—was to delineate areas that flowed organically and that related stylistically to one another. The place needed warmth and depth, so it wouldn't feel cavernous and undecorated and impersonal, a common problem with large-scale rooms.

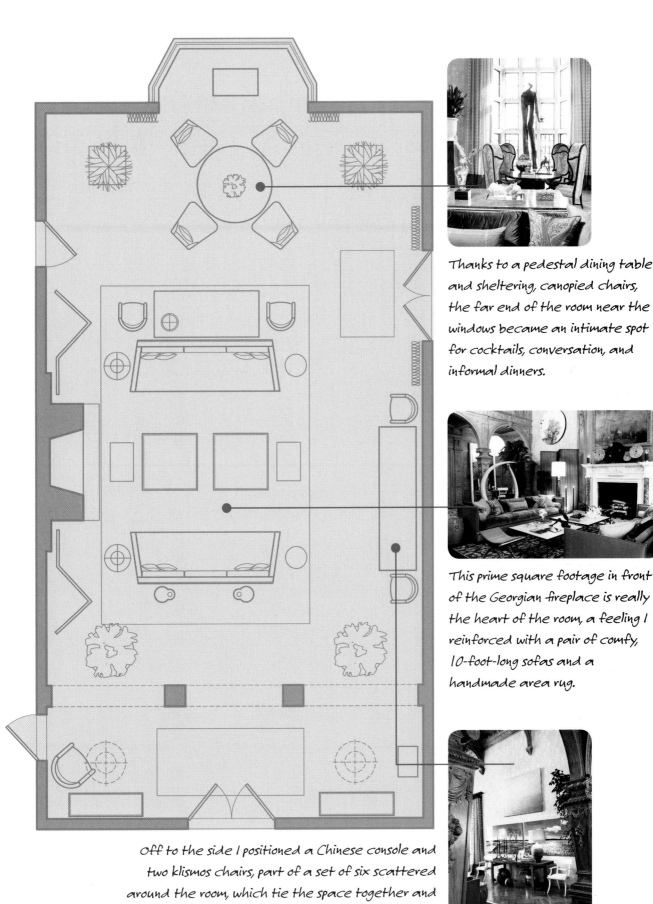

Thanks to a pedestal dining table and sheltering, canopied chairs, the far end of the room near the windows became an intimate spot for cocktails, conversation, and informal dinners.

This prime square footage in front of the Georgian fireplace is really the heart of the room, a feeling I reinforced with a pair of comfy, 10-foot-long sofas and a handmade area rug.

Off to the side I positioned a Chinese console and two klismos chairs, part of a set of six scattered around the room, which tie the space together and offer additional seating when needed.

A loosened-up layout and easily moved furniture that's at home in any part of the room encourages socializing.

Since the room had only a single window, I used landscape paintings to fake an outdoor view. Going frameless helps create an unstuffy vibe.

HEIGHT MAKES RIGHT

When walls stretch 29 feet high, there need to be gradual visual transitions between you and the ceiling, or you'll feel small and insignificant. To bring the room's towering proportions down to a more human scale, I used a bronze sculpture and a plant on a pedestal, *opposite*, that help bridge the distance to the ceiling. That's also why I stacked the artwork, *right*.

Canopied wing chairs
form personal
cocoons of coziness.

No great room would be complete without faux mastodon tusks. Cheeky, irreverent, and head-turning, they're a fun way to accessorize if you're redoing your estate.

MAKING ARRANGEMENTS

Formal groupings with matched sets of furniture don't have to feel buttoned up—if you keep the look loose and limber. This fireplace vignette draws from tradition but feels modern, thanks to an eclectic mix of materials and styles. Upholstering each of the ten-foot custom sofas in two different fabrics—silk denim and silk velvet—prevents them from feeling overly massive, even as they anchor the grouping. The orange leather Italian stools are nimble enough to move around depending on the occasion and the number of guests—and add a bold pop of color.

Hinged screens crafted from vintage
safety glass reinforce the room's
provocative mix of styles and centuries.

TIP #2 : Light up your life

Lighting is an afterthought in a lot of rooms. And in some rooms, it's given zero thought. I swear that every guy we helped on *Queer Eye* owned the same torchiere, with a blazing 200-watt bulb intended to illuminate the entire room. It was a lot of pressure on a single lamp (not to mention a fire hazard), and it was so blindingly bright, it was otherworldly, like something out of *Poltergeist*—"Go into the light, Carol Ann, go into the light!" Not attractive.

People tend to shoehorn lighting in at the end of the decorating process (and at the end of budget, assuming there's still a budget at the end), randomly adding a floor lamp here or a table lamp there and cheaping out on the lampshades. But that's a missed opportunity to make a dramatic statement, because lighting is equal to the layout and the color scheme in its transformative powers—which is why you need to think about it at the same time you're doing your furniture plan and palette. Lighting is instrumental in determining how a room feels. Think of a chic restaurant with its votive-lit banquette tables and darkened alcoves, and the sexy vibe that creates. Or think of a typical supermarket with its evenly distributed, superbright fluorescents that don't cast any shadows. It scores a zero in the atmosphere department but a hundred for what it's supposed to do—make food shopping easy and user-friendly. Two totally different kinds of lighting, two totally different effects. One is emotion-producing and the other practical and convenient.

GLOW AND BEHOLD

Whether it's quiet and under-the-radar or brazen and look-at-me, lighting can set the tone for the entire room. A custom fixture, *opposite*, of interlocking restoration glass reinforces the furniture's clean geometric lines and delivers high-wattage flair. The lamps, *above*, are far more subtle, with barely-there shapes that let the refined furniture shine.

This angular, steel-and-glass custom fixture has a spare silhouette but enough visual heft to make a stunning statement, which is why I use it so often in my designs.

hoosing the right lighting for a room or a space involves striking a balance between form, function, and overall design and effect. While you want to be able to see, you also want to set an appropriate mood and have the fixture either be an attractive design element or not be visible. There are three main types of lighting: general, task, and accent. General is for everyday, overall use, and with the use of a plug-in or installed dimmer, it can go from general lighting to generally delicious lighting. Task light is about illuminating areas for a specific need: under-the-counter lights help you cook your favorite meal, a desk lamp beside your computer allows you to send e-mails without squinting, a floor lamp beside an armchair lets you curl up with your favorite book. Fitted with dimmers or three-way bulbs, task lights can be an integral component to the atmosphere of the room. Accent light is mostly for mood, like an uplight behind a ficus tree, picture lights mounted over artwork, a sconce in a hallway, or a small lamp on an entrance hall table. Aim for a layered mix of all three types and build your lighting program from the floor up. Start with uplights, then progress to floor lamps, tabletop lighting, wall sconces, and finally ceiling fixtures. Use more lights than you think you need but at a lower wattage. So instead of three light fixtures of 100 watts each, go for seven fixtures with 40-watt bulbs. And don't run extension cords all over the place. Just make a call to an electrician, add some new outlets and switches, and the room will look brilliant.

SOME ILLUMINATING IDEAS

Why settle for uninteresting light fixtures (like the kind that usually come preinstalled in a place) when there are stylish options that marry function with flair? These overheads, *above*, are a contemporary updating of Shaker simplicity that mirror the home's trimwork. A trio of no-nonsense outdoor carriage lights, *opposite*, enhances the rusticity of my rural lake house.

These shepherd's hook carriage lights look lifted from an English manor house and then modernized, but I scored them for about $50 apiece at a home-improvement store.

To accentuate a hallway in the VIP pavilion at the World's Fair in Japan, I installed these rectangular light boxes, which purposely resemble shoji screens.

FLIP FOR THE LIGHTS FANTASTIC

Treat lighting like sculpture, and the style payoff can be huge. In a windowless hallway, *above*, long, narrow light boxes staggered at different heights put a chic spin on traditional wall sconces. Lit from within, a glowing built-in light box/ console, *opposite*, becomes a museum-worthy display cabinet for an easily changeable array of artwork, vases, and books.

Don't always default to an opaque shade. This see-through mesh, installed at the ultrachic W Hotel–Westwood I designed in LA, lets the bulb, filament, and supports become stripped-back design elements.

This built-in is a lesson in creative problem solving: I constructed it to craftily disguise an unsightly jog in the wall and wound up with some spectacular uplighting.

Next to a well-sharpened set of knives, there's nothing an at-home chef appreciates more than restaurant-quality lighting for cooking and dimmers for entertaining.

RISE AND SHINE

In the kitchen, strive to go beyond the utilitarian and look for inspiration in illumination. In this Manhattan loft, *right*, I needed a substantial fixture to counterbalance the enormous marble-topped island—and wimpy overheads weren't going to cut it. Soaring cathedral ceilings in this beach house, *opposite*, necessitated four different types of lighting: from under-counter to hanging boxes to circular surface mounts to window pendants, all superstylish and showstopping.

I had this custom-fiberglass and steel-frame light box manufactured to the same dimensions as the island below it.

Dimmers allow these box fixtures to be as versatile as they are distinctive, alternating between bright task lights and nighttime mood enhancers.

TIP #3 : Color your world (sort of)

Deciding on a room's color scheme is intimidating to most people. Mostly they choose colors that are unadventurous rather than colors that make them happy. They agonize over all the choices, fretting about finding the just-right shade among the thousands of paint chips and fabric swatches—and then, because of this daunting experience, they end up with off-white, a cocktail, and an Advil. But it doesn't have to be such an angst-ridden ordeal. Taking color cues from your wardrobe and favorite objects is a great first step in discovering colors that you gravitate toward and have a connection with. And it's always my strategy when people are unable to narrow down their selections of possible colors—which happens on almost every episode of *Dress My Nest*.

But after you choose the colors, how should you use the hues? On the walls, the rug, the sofa, the appliances? My advice, and I use it in every room I create, is to employ a two-part strategy: start with a classic, grounded color for the backdrop, then introduce splashes of bold color as accents to give the space some oomph. The reason this technique is so effective is that in my lexicon, classic colors aren't just confined to boring beige and tired taupe. Instead, I rely on a nuanced palette that has longevity, that never disappoints, and that can swing traditional and modern and anywhere in between. My personal list of timeless, timely hues—call them Thom's Pick-and-Stick Neutrals—includes twenty shades from sweatshirt gray to Nantucket fog to soft fern to Branchport brown (see the complete list on page 57). With these as the base, you have the beginnings of a fail-safe room that always feels clean-lined, untrendy, and beautiful and is able to coexist peacefully with almost any *other* color you want to add, from Chinese red to Hermès orange to teal blue. Trust me: it will all work.

YOUR PRIMARY COLOR PRINCIPLES

Establish a pared-down palette, and you can then introduce colors in surprising, potent combinations. An entryway with unobtrusive off-white walls, *above*, enables an exquisite blue Tiffany lampshade of leaded glass, a dark-green Japanese vase, pink peonies, and orange chair to harmonize without matching. An otherwise-neutral living room, *opposite*, gets a jolt from a tangerine pillow, burnt-sienna lampshade, and a coffee table with a Chinese-red lacquered interior.

The colors in a room shouldn't overwhelm the artwork—and vice versa. These gradations of indigo that incrementally fade into yellow are soothing, not jarring, and don't disrupt the understated feel created by the furniture and rug.

Look for unexpected places to sneak in a color surprise—like this Chinese-red lacquer on the inside of the coffee table.

AN APPROACH SO COOL, IT'S HOT

Just outside this oceanfront Miami condo are all the intense, tropical hues of South Beach, from sizzling turquoise to vibrant flamingo pink. As an antidote to those saturated colors, the owner wanted rooms with a crisp, modern palette that didn't feel austere. The solution: snowy marble floors and walls warmed up by light-blue, aqua, and cinnamon-orange hues. In the living room, I introduced color via a pair of 1920s French chairs (the cinnamon-orange), a low-slung sofa (the ice-blue), and a coffee table with a tiled top (the aqua). Breezy but sophisticated accents—striped cotton pillows, palm fronds in a vase, artwork with a beach scene—reinforce the casual-yet-contemporary theme.

Throw pillows are an inexpensive, low-commitment way to bring some pops of color to a room. These richly striped pillows echo the hues in the painting, and the dhurrie fabric is easy-care and kid-friendly.

This red has amazing vitality and versatility. Its deep richness works with refined spaces, but it also has vibrant zip, so it gives a room energy.

THE SECRET TO BEING WELL RED

Nothing rivals red for creating drama. Confident, racy, and exciting, the right red is eye-catching and stimulating. Increase its potency by using it sparingly—as a quick hit of color on a door or a floor, on a pillow or a throw—rather than drenching an entire room. For example, these Asian-style lanterns, *opposite*, punctuate an otherwise color-free, minimalist desk. If you do want to use red more liberally, then opt for timeless pieces with classic shapes, like these traditional leather wing chairs, *right*. Because either the color or the shape needs to be bold—not both.

BENJAMIN MOORE
DEEP ROSE

Upholstered in crimson leather, two pared-down wing chairs create a sexy, secluded dining spot in a New York apartment. A marble-topped table with silvery branch legs heightens the theatricality and contrasts with the angular chairs.

To bring some oomph to a Zen-style desk, I added hurricane sconces in glossy Chinese red.

This is such a balanced, meditative blue. It's earthy and fresh with a clarity that's therapeutic.

FARROW & BALL
COOK'S BLUE

This seaweed-green vintage glass lamp borrows color cues from the pillow's abstract floral print and Hamptons beaches.

OUT OF THE BLUE

Blue is one of my dependable, go-to hues. I use it to bring serenity, peacefulness, and airiness to spaces. This shade works especially well in undersized rooms, because it conveys a sense of the expansiveness of the sky and sea. It can be an ideal accent, like this patterned pillow, *right*, or as the color for an entire room or part of a room, like this stairwell, *opposite*.

For this Hamptons guesthouse, the blue stairwell is a transition zone, signaling you're descending down to the watery tranquility of the pool.

The same way clothes should be wearable, colors should be livable. These twenty tints are calm, fluid, and dependably stylish no matter the decor.

MY TRIED-AND-TRUE HUES

Nearly every room I've ever created includes at least one of the twenty Benjamin Moore colors on the opposite page. These shades are my version of neutrals, the background colors I consistently use for walls, floors, furniture, and fabric. They range from a white the color of porcelain to a muted brown just this side of tobacco. Use any of these, and you'll have a solid base that's sophisticated, timeless, and modern without being chilly or overpowering.

There's no rule that says furniture can't be two-toned. Pair beige and gray suede on a single chair, and you get a look that's doubly rich and inviting.

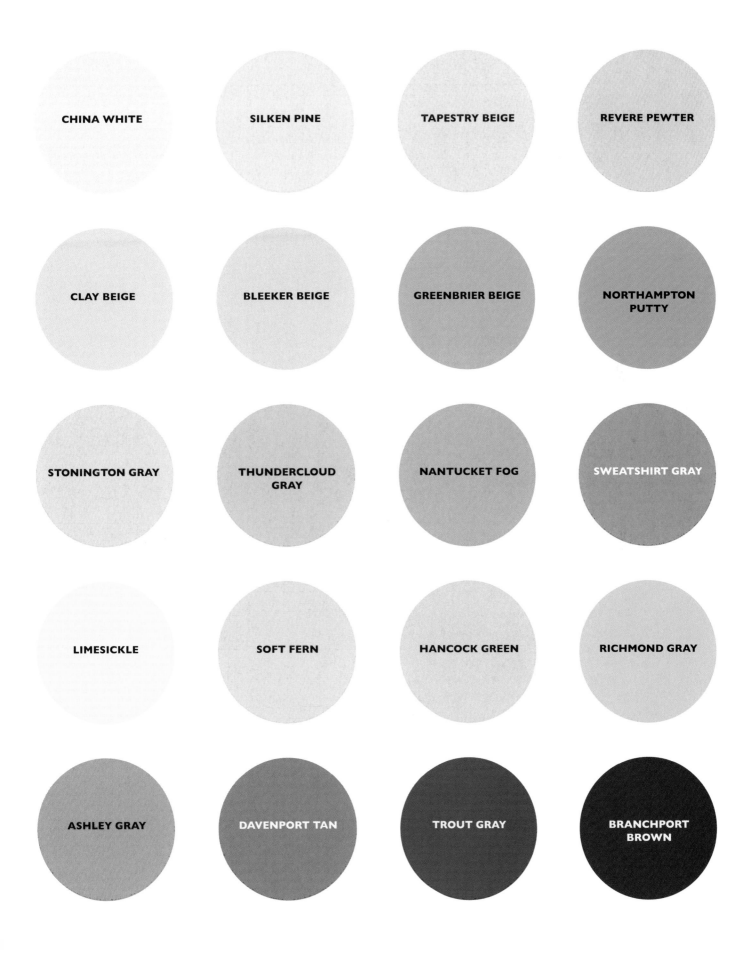

CHINA WHITE

SILKEN PINE

TAPESTRY BEIGE

REVERE PEWTER

CLAY BEIGE

BLEEKER BEIGE

GREENBRIER BEIGE

NORTHAMPTON PUTTY

STONINGTON GRAY

THUNDERCLOUD GRAY

NANTUCKET FOG

SWEATSHIRT GRAY

LIMESICKLE

SOFT FERN

HANCOCK GREEN

RICHMOND GRAY

ASHLEY GRAY

DAVENPORT TAN

TROUT GRAY

BRANCHPORT BROWN

Comforting, nonstimulating shades of biscuit, oatmeal, and linen keep the look serene and grounded.

COLOR FULL

Picking colors isn't just about selecting paint chips. When I put together a room's palette, I factor in everything from the tones of the woods to the weaves of the fabric, to the sheen of the metals, to the glaze on the ceramics. This collection of materials, *left*, was my color starter kit for the living room on the opposite page. The palette was kicked off with the rough-hewn, reclaimed barn beams that span the ceiling. All of the other neutrals dominoed from there, including the abaca armchairs, the rug, and even the books stacked on the coffee table.

Salvaged antique barn beams, with all their hand-hewn imperfections, add instant history to a new-construction space. The timber's timeworn patina was the pivot point for the room's subdued colors.

To prevent neutrals from seeming flat, they need something to react against. These provocatively hued chartreuse vases totally make the room.

Painting the ceiling, radiator, fireplace, and trim a brighter white than the walls gives them an appealing sharpness. It also creates the kind of slight visual tension necessary in a color-free room.

A WHITER SHADE OF PALE

White is a modernist mainstay. It reflects light, can unify disparate styles, and makes a claustrophobic room feel spacious. But since stark white can feel clinical, try more welcoming shades, like meringue, tapioca, pearl, coconut, and milk. For crispness, partner with dark woods and abaca rugs.

The high-contrast combo of black and white always looks debonair—think of Cary Grant in a tux. Get the look with oversized photos in coal-colored frames and a leather and blackened-steel X-based chair.

Treat vegetation as decoration. The frilly fronds on this fern are like cascading, free-form sculpture and provide a hit of greenery and all-natural color.

PUT IT IN NEUTRAL

Rooms without loud-and-proud hues can still have plenty of personality—as long as there are standout pieces and strong textural contrasts, like in this shore house living room. Paneling the walls and the built-in cabinetry introduces character and warmth, while a sisal rug underfoot is tactile and beachy (and hides all the sand that's inevitably tracked in). A pair of sophisticated, mid-century Dunbar ottomans upholstered in a refined wool function as extra seating and are a counterpoint to the more casual, tile-topped coffee table. The simple matchstick blinds, an exotic hammered metal lamp, and posh silk pillows in a steel blue introduce a mélange of tactile surfaces and divergent moods.

The curves of the circular coffee table mitigate all the sharp angles of the sofas and ottomans, and the tiled top is laid-back compared to the more formal furniture.

TIP #4 : There's truth in the texture

Rooms need an abundance of textures. And I don't mean drunk people who won't go home. Interiors lacking a rich variety of tactile, touchable sensations feel flat—literally. To achieve the best balance of textures in a room, always remember that opposites attack—which is exactly what you want. Textures that fight one another produce visual tension, and that combativeness makes a room more interesting. In every interior, try to partner up rough with smooth, shiny with matte, sleek with antique. The floor, as the largest surface in the room, is a great place to introduce interesting texture. Reclaimed wood, smooth concrete, rugged stone, and even leather tiles underfoot can provide texture from the ground up. Adding tactile rugs—everything from wool kilim to plush chenille to nubby abaca—introduces another layer of textural depth.

Use unexpected textures in unconventional ways. A refined demilune table wrapped in rope, a lampshade crafted from metal mesh, and a petrified log used as an accent table are all creative ways to incorporate texture into an interior. Nature's a top-notch source for sustainable—and affordable—textural treasures to counteract all the glass and metal and plastics of twenty-first-century life. Think of grasscloth walls, a driftwood lamp, an organic wood bowl filled with seashells found along your favorite beach. The world is your oyster shell when it comes to texture, so take advantage of it.

BUILDING BLOCKS OF STYLE

Intermingling a wide variety of unusual textures gives this living room, *above* and *opposite*, its refined-meets-raw sensibility. Concrete floors painted a pristine white, exposed bricks bordered by classic trimwork, and handcrafted wallpaper with textural fibers provide the industrial-elegant foundation. Then I added light-blond oak Italian chairs upholstered in zigzagging cut velvet and suede and a rug pieced from antique kilims, with a 1960s stag in buffed aluminum as the crowning touch.

Outlining the fireplace's brick in traditional trimwork plays up the contrast between rough and smooth, polished and plain.

Hipsters may have co-opted the taxidermy trend, but a cool vintage piece, like this forty-year-old metal mounted stag, is forever chic.

Next time you're stumped about what to do with a room, try closing your eyes and imagining how you really want the room to feel.

YOU'VE GOT THE TOUCH

On the surface, all of these textures—bronze linen patterned with gold silk, ink-bleed fibrous wallpaper, suede, cut velvet, crewelwork on linen, stitched wool kilims— wouldn't seem to form a cohesive whole, but that's the point. These opposing textures give the room liveliness, and their related palette and graphic patterns prevent them from feeling discordant.

Don't discount lampshades—like this bristly coconut-hair number—when you're looking to inject some texture into a room.

Nailhead trim toughens up the sumptuous blue suede on this custom French Fort bench I designed.

Neutral rooms loaded with tactile zing seem drenched in color— but better.

Layered window treatments create privacy—and additional layers of texture. Here, semisheer linen curtains and bark shades continue the all-natural vibe that dominates throughout the room.

ONCE AGAIN, WITH FEELING

Look for unexpected places to add texture. A rope-wrapped accent table, sustainably harvested sea fans, and a shimmery mercury glass lamp, *right*, transform the typical dining room display into a tactile tableau. Rustic, Wide-plank pine floors, *opposite*, aren't always the first choice in a high-traffic kitchen. But they age beautifully and provide a warm counterpoint to stainless-steel appliances.

Mixing restaurant-grade stainless-steel appliances with rustic, weathered furnishings creates a striking visual tension.

Love this slate surround and locally quarried stone. With the bleached wood beams, it gives the room haute rustic appeal.

A timeworn carpenter's bench gets a second life as a self-service bar. With its pre-dinged and pockmarked surface, any new drink stain just adds to the patina.

THE LAKE EFFECT

My 1930s-era lake house is a texture extravaganza filled with incongruous but fabulous combinations: pine V-grooved paneling stained gray, a two-story stone fireplace, salvaged wood beams, bluestone floors, linen and cotton-velvet upholstery, and sculptural Italian wicker lamps. The informal mix echoes the laid-back approach I have to the place. Every weekend in summer (and spring and fall), there's a steady stream of guests traipsing barefoot from the house to the boat dock outside, usually with cocktail in hand. There's no pretentiousness here, and I wanted to reflect that in the decor. The sturdy, stain-hiding fabrics can handle damp bathing suits and wet dogs but are still stylish enough to keep the look from devolving into lake shack clichés.

With a fireplace this earthy and attention-getting, you don't need to do much more to create drama—although the papier-mâché ram's head doesn't hurt.

COMBINATIONS FOUND IN NATURE

Unlike colors, it's almost impossible for textures to clash. No matter how different they are, they're almost always companionable. So don't be afraid to go full throttle with the variety and the volume. *Left*, a rope-covered demilune table, shell globe light, intricate wood paneling, and massive floor mirror all manage to comfortably inhabit the same corner; this one-of-a-kind, hand-glazed tile table, *below*, embedded with fossil-style leaves, is set with a smooth-turned Japanese wood bowl and artisan ceramic dishes; at my lake house, *opposite*, relaxed lounge chairs upholstered in cotton velvet sit beside a pair of Italian gourd-shaped wicker floor lamps. Three different textural mash-ups, three completely different and striking looks.

Wrapped in rope, this demilune table provides striking textural contrast to all the mahogany on the walls and undercuts the formality of the Gothic paneling.

Sculptural during the day, these loosely woven wicker lamps cast intriguing shadows when lit at night.

Look-alike porcelain replicas of endangered coral are as tactile as the real deal but a lot more eco-responsible.

WHERE THE BUOYS ARE

Too many beach interiors go overboard with the olde nautical decor, like diving helmet clocks and schooner wheel mirrors. But at this Hamptons home, the maritime chic is understated, with subtle textures and a reserved palette that hint at the shore locale. In the living room fireplace, *right*, that translated into a surround of ceramic tiles with undulating, three-dimensional waves and a bronze sconce that mimics both the carapace of a crustacean and the ridges on seashells.

Beach-house rugs attract sand and can look heavy on steamy summer days. A better choice: hardwood floors with an inlay that mimics a carpet, like this circular herringbone outlined with ebony.

IT'S ALL ON THE SURFACE

When color is at a minimum, texture needs to be at a maximum. It prevents a neutral room from feeling washed out and brings some zing to monochromatic interiors. This trio of beach house rooms shows the power of substituting textures for color: it looks like rattan, *left*, but this woven chair is crafted from strips of leather, which crisps up pure white cushions; in a small powder room, *below*, squares of beadboard hung vertically and horizontally are as dramatic as any wildly hued wallpaper; understated shades of ecru, oatmeal, and fern, *opposite*, feel far richer surrounded by a woven wool rug, rattan wing chair, and distressed-pine coffee table.

An upholstered footstool can become an impromptu coffee table with the addition of an oversized rattan tray.

Rimmed in metal and dangling on a leather strap, this porthole-style mirror is a textural double threat.

Faux ibex horns that look to be direct from the African savanna interact gracefully with all the worn woods.

Natural jute and abaca rugs can sometimes be too scratchy for toddlers. Swap for a wool look-alike that's soft under little toes.

With raised reliefs that mimic seedpods, hives, and nettles, Danish ceramist Axel Salto's decorative pottery brings even more tactile surfaces to the room.

ALL HANDS ON DECK

A medley of textures, some simple and some sophisticated, give this living room its offhandedly elegant feel. All the tactile surfaces harmonize, balancing each other so that no single texture overwhelms, allowing each to contribute equally to the fresh, traditional decor. Like the posh oak and woven suede stools, which echo the colors of the modest rattan blinds. Or the glossy oak coffee table topped with hand-split bamboo, which contrasts with the fireplace's matte herringbone tiles. A hammered bronze floor lamp with a whipstitched shade, ceramic sculptures, and graphic wool rug round out the polished, pulled-together look.

Less obvious than seashells, these ceramic sculptures are like stylized versions of spiny sea urchins.

TIP #5 : Lose the matchy-matchiness

Pulling together a room's decor is a lot like getting dressed. When you put on your clothes every day, you don't wear a single brand from head to toe (or at least, I *hope* you don't). Instead, you mix it up. A well-dressed guy might combine a vintage wool Brooks Brothers blazer, dark-indigo jeans, a hand-tooled leather belt, an over-sized men's watch inherited from his grandfather, and a cashmere sweater scored at a designer outlet. The final outfit is sophisticated and laid back—and unmistakably his own. That same distinctive chic should also be happening in your interiors. Each piece you select should have character, be eye-catching, and tell your story. It doesn't matter if your furniture, artwork, and textiles are collected during exotic, around-the-world trips or are sourced from

local design shops within twenty miles of your home, as long as the overall look is original, with intriguing juxtapositions and unexpected contrasts. Because a clean-lined IKEA sofa next to a sinuous, hand-carved Balinese chair atop an antique kilim rug is a lot more visually compelling than an IKEA couch with an IKEA chair and an IKEA rug. Not to knock the Swedish chain's cheap-chic aesthetic (which I love), but its pieces look exponentially better when they're partnered with furniture that doesn't require assembly with a wrench.

Keep in mind that I'm not suggesting a random mishmash of stuff. What you're after instead is a nondecorated look that's coordinated but not contrived. There should be subtle repetition of colors and shapes, symmetrical groupings, and commonalities among objects. A Greek-key print on a pillow should reiterate the geometric pattern on the border of a curtain, which should echo the crosshatching mesh of a wire Bertoia chair. Because if it's totally matchy-matchy, it looks starchy and decorated, but if it's all casually connected, it looks stylish.

MIX MASTER

Diverse doesn't mean discordant. Although you would never find the furniture in either of these interiors as a suite in a showroom, the overall look is harmonious and head-turning. At my lake house, *opposite*, the chairs don't match, but their similarities—wood construction, open backs, patterned fabric seats—bring cohesiveness to the dining area. *Above*, the low-contrast color scheme and similar profile tie together sofas, carved Balinese chairs, and accent tables.

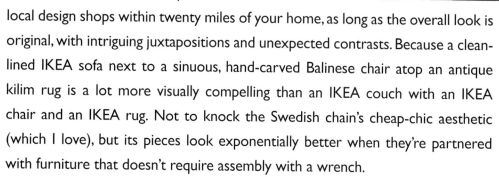

These high-backed, angular chairs might not seem the most obvious choice for a casual 1930s lake house, but their see-through silhouette allows for uninterrupted views of the water.

Identical abaca rugs, one here in the sitting area and the other underneath the nearby pool table, visually relate the room's two activity zones.

Dramatic red flame coral injects a note of vibrant color.

TWO IF BY SEA

In this East Coast beach house, what could have been a disjointed hodgepodge—cane and rattan chairs, a wooden sugar press turned accent table, Asian-style lantern lamps and an industrial coffee table crafted from train rail—feels totally connected, thanks to a controlled repetition of hues. The black ebonized cane chairs match the base of the coffee table, and the color of the tan cushions is repeated in the cerused oak base of the sofa and the rattan chairs positioned to the left. The tones of the abaca rug are repeated in those same rattan chairs and the window blinds. Touches of the Far East—the Chinese console behind the couch, Japanese pottery, an Asian deer sculpture—also unify the space.

These graphic striped pillows replicate the weave pattern of the rattan chairs, just in an exaggerated, abstract way.

Lit like costly sculptures, a pair of humble antlers cast shadows as intriguing as any artwork.

GETTING THE HANG OF IT

There's an art to arranging an eye-pleasing composition of artwork, accessories, and furniture. Don't overdo any one mood, material, or movement, and know that it will take some tweaking and rejiggering to hit on the most compatible grouping. This trio, *left*, works because the spareness of the pieces—vintage antler mounts bleached of color and a Gavin Ziegler mixed media combining paint and stock certificates—highlights their differences. There's a relaxed randomness, *below*, to this mix of hyperrealistic landscapes, branch-shaped candelabra, and framed photos.

Looking fabulous is purpose enough for some pieces. Although you can't sit on them or store anything in them, these wooden spheres deliver major organic chic.

An unpredictable mix—a Caio Fonseca abstract painting, a low Lucite-legged console I designed, a 1920s French deco chair, and twin fiberglass lamps—is multilayered but refined, with no jarring colors or shapes.

TIP #6: The smaller the space, the bigger the risk

I love, love, love powder rooms. They're these exquisite little jewel boxes that you give to your guests, and they should be just over-the-top fabulous. And why not? Since it doesn't need to be a practical space for day-to-day living, let it be a showstopper. Guests should open the door and be like, *Wow, this is cool!* The same principle applies to all of the smaller spaces in your house with wow-moment potential—the foyers, the hallways, the breakfast nooks, the pantry, and any other room that has a specific, special purpose that's not part of your everyday routine. These are the spots where you can be exuberant and maximalist and do expensive decor on a budget because you have less square footage to cover.

Choose effects that are impractical and fun. Maybe that's a silver-leafed ceiling or a decorative forest panorama hand-painted on the wall. The best part is that you don't have to do something all that outlandish to make a strong statement in a small space. Try turning a hallway into a gallery, with rows of artwork illuminated by picture lights. Paint the ceiling a saturated, notice-me color, like a deep, deep charcoal, or lay a look-twice antique runner with a graphic pattern. All of these can utterly change the feel and the mood of a room and make it seem much larger than its actual dimensions. It's like the way a short person with a big personality seems taller—think Napoleon or Danny DeVito.

Remember that small is your invitation to be bold, brash, and adventurous. Don't shrink from the challenge.

THE HOUSE THAT ROARED

Crazy-exuberant floral fabric turned this teeny W Hotel–Westwood cabana, *above*, into a fab chill-out zone—don't you want to hang out and sip an umbrella drink? My Manhattan apartment, *opposite*, isn't much bigger, so I went with an equally radical plan: knock down the wall between the living room and bedroom and install factory-grade safety glass.

Not many homeowners would replace a perfectly good wall with one made from safety glass. But this unconventional swap gives my apartment just the right balance of urban, sophisticated, and fun.

If the most adventurous item in your powder room is scented soap, it's time to branch out. An arboreal mural, *opposite*, lends a forest feel to my rural lake house bathroom. I liked the safety glass from my Manhattan digs so much that I repeated it in the apartment's powder room, *below*, but I went even more over-the-top by backing it with a refined antiqued mirror. Lattice loses any garden connotations, *left*, when partnered with tongue-in-chic wallpaper created by Studio Printworks in Manhattan and imprinted with all-terrain SUVs and layered over a mirror.

There are a lot more original options than off-the-shelf vanities. Even a felled sycamore plank can be transformed into an eco-friendly bathroom counter.

A modern sconce shakes up the woodland wallpaper, tempering the pattern so it seems elegant, not earthy.

A staggered artwork arrangement—a carved-wood head mounted up high, a framed print, and a retro clock hung progressively lower—keeps the eye roving more than a static, symmetrical grouping would.

THE INN CROWD

Boutique hotels are experts at squeezing a lot of style into a small space. My redesign for this West Coast hotel is chock full of reusable ideas: a contemporary headboard that extends clear to the ceiling, *opposite*, turns the bed into a dramatic focal point. A desk at a right angle to the console table, *above*, carves out a separate, defined area for work and dining.

Reflections from this colossal mirror blur the boundaries of the room, making it feel larger.

To prevent a raftered dormer from seeming too rustic, disrupt it with some decorous touches: a crisp chevron-patterned rug and an Asian-inspired platform bed.

OVER THE TOP

Originally a ramshackle chicken barn, the cozy guest cottage at my lake house has been transformed into a sophisticated version of summer camp—think high-style Hiawatha. Here in the small, second-floor sleeping dormer—accessible by ladder and rope—I kept the original rafters intact but exposed only a few inches of the beams, so that it wouldn't feel too attic-y. Stained white, the ten-inch pine planks on the floor add to the easy, breezy feel.

Since the slanted, paneled, two-color ceiling has so much going on visually, I opted for simple furniture with sass, like this clean-cut table in zesty lemon-yellow lacquer.

A pink headboard is pure flirty fun, but
the industrial-style pharmacy lamps on
the nightstands temper the sweetness.
A woven rush stool that guests use as a
luggage rack looks attractive even
when off duty.

TIP #7 : Clashing is dashing

In my designs, the stars are stripes. And so are the paisleys, chevrons, checks, arabesques, and florals, occasionally all at the same time. Mixing patterns, especially those that initially seem to be incompatible, is one of my hallmarks—and it can be one of yours, too. Graphic, clashing prints energize a space, and when they're layered, the wow factor gets cranked up even more. The technique isn't new—in the period between the world wars, it was almost mandatory for upholstery in English country houses to include not-matching chintz and hunting plaids—but it still feels totally fresh and inventive today.

Pulling it off does take some discipline. The mix should be intentional, not accidental, so don't just throw random patterns in a room and hope for the best. (Hint: If guests ask if you decorated the room while in a hungover haze, that's a sign you missed the mark.) Always vary the scale of the prints—a pillow with small dots beside a pillow with oversized florals works better than teensy dots beside teensy florals—and try to have commonality between the colors. What you're aiming for is a playful equilibrium that keeps the eye engaged and moving, which is why this is a supereffective method for making small spaces seem larger.

PUT IT IN PRINT

The vibe at my lake house is easygoing, and that extends to the outdoor decor, *above*. Since the house is painted a blue-slate gray with barnyard-red trim and there's so much color from the greenery and the water, I wanted the fabrics for this daybed to hold their own. A vintage Indian textile with a dense pattern provides the base; a pair of pillows in similar hues with an exaggerated abstract floral deliver the punch line.

At the Greystone Estate, the dialogue between all the different prints works because none of them is shouting. From the wallpaper to the drapes to the canopied chair upholstery, the colors are muted and the prints are quietly elegant.

The glossy red of these lacquered cubes pops against the brown-white carpet.

FLOOR SHOW

People are often hesitant about buying a patterned rug. They're afraid it will limit their choices of fabrics and furniture. But a carefully considered print underfoot can galvanize the entire look of a room, becoming a dynamic jumping-off point. At the World's Fair pavilion in Japan, the square footage I had to cover was huge. A plain single-color carpet would have been too visually heavy, but this pattern, with its interlocking and overlapping octagons and squares, is crisp and classically modern. It's almost like a neutral but a lot more interesting. Sticking with the same palette, I found a subtle chevron pattern for the lounge chair and then turned up the volume slightly with the striped seat cushion. Sofa pillows in the same fabric continue the stripe motif and turn it on its side.

96

Leave the ocelot and leopard spots back in the '80s. The freshest way to display is more naturalistic and less hedonistic.

Hung in a three-over-three grid, these framed prints creatively take the place of a headboard.

PARTY ANIMALS

Heed the call of the wild and add some of Mother Nature's finest fauna to your decor. At my lake house, framed animal prints have the run of the place but are well-tamed enough to play well with other patterns. In the guest bedroom, *right*, antique-look illustrations echo the exoticism of an Indian tapestry bedspread.

In the media corner of the living room, a buck mount, framed insect studies, and avian pillows create a real animal-house effect. It all works because of the refined lines of the sophisticated sofa and end tables.

Yes, it's a bird—I'm nothing if not consistent.

TIP #8 : Every room needs a surprise

I'm a big fan of upending expectations. While at first glance the rooms I design don't seem so out-there—there aren't any surreal, lip-shaped sofas or fluorescent-pink pendant lamps—there's always some winking wit involved. Like the taxidermy deer at my lake house with the unlit cigarette dangling from its mouth. Or the Emmy statue that I use as a toilet-paper holder for my Manhattan powder room. Or that orange rubber lobster I stuck in a rococo frame and hung as impromptu artwork in my first postcollege apartment. Visual shenanigans like these prevent interiors from being staid and predictable and showcase your sense of humor, even if it's sometimes as outlandish as mine.

Taking pieces out of context or using them in daring ways is one of my go-to strategies for adding some surprise to a space. Installing utilitarian galvanized-metal outdoor lights inside a home throws a curveball to the conventional. Treating enormous industrial cogs as sculpture, hanging classic-looking wallpaper that on closer inspection has a repeating pattern of small SUVs, or replacing a wall with safety glass plays with preconceived notions and jolts a room out of a same-old, same-old rut.

Not sticking to the predictable is a surefire method to bring some excitement to apartments and starter homes that lack interesting architectural details. Guests won't notice that you're living in a small Sheetrock box if you shake things up with off-kilter touches that keep them guessing. Even just painting an interior door or accent wall a bold color, like fire-engine red, can be a hey-that's-cool surprise. Wherever and whenever, search for ways to tweak the traditional, enliven the expected, and attempt something off-the-wall—especially if it's on the wall.

FOWL PLAY

Maybe it's my inner ornithologist, but I always seem to add birds to my interiors—it's no wonder my design how-to show is called *Dress My Nest*. These inexpensive plastic critters, *above*, are some of the funnest I've found. Walk past or make a sudden move, and their motion sensors trigger species-specific birdsong—think of it as cheep chic.

Instead of going with the expected and suspending a trophy-sized marlin in this beach house foyer, I hung supersized industrial cogs. They're fresh, fun, and amazingly sculptural.

A circular rug echoes the shape of the machinery.

A stitched-leather door with nailhead trim was inspired by the Arts and Crafts movement, and the exaggerated, ebonized door frame by 1940s Hollywood.

AMERICAN PLANKSTER

Even the most buttoned-up of spaces can have some visual twists. This pavilion I created at the Japanese World's Fair was for diplomats and dignitaries to meet and mingle. Not only was it supposed to be elegant, sophisticated, and inviting, but it also had to showcase the best in American craftsmanship and design. I started with classic elements with a modern twist, including: a wool carpet with an octagonal trellis pattern; my custom-made, square-armed Saratoga sofa; coffee tables topped with Vermont stone; and velvet-upholstered slipper chairs. Then I added a striking room divider created by Bryan Nash Gill and constructed of ten-foot-long slabs of felled sycamore. But rather than doing precise planks, we kept the wood as-is, with all of the rawness and unevenness intact. Floor lamps with metal-mesh shades that riff on classic candelabra and a trio of conversation-starter sculptures constructed from circular machine parts also liven up the space. The finished look redefines Americana in a contemporary way.

This chair's silhouette is classic, but upholstering it in two different graphic patterns loosens up its traditionalism.

OH SAY CAN YOU SEA

Sometimes the surprise isn't the objects in a room, it's how you use them. This apartment in Miami's South Beach has unbelievable views of the Atlantic, and to make the most of them, I wanted a clean, unencumbered white box that turned the scenery outside into a major design element. To do that, I skipped window treatments and curtained the interior walls with white drapes, which creates the illusion of being inside a glass box. It's a departure from the norm—you know what they say about people in glass houses?—which is why I love it. The floor plan I chose was also atypical. Floating a pair of my custom linen chaises in opposite directions in the middle of the space is an unusual move that tends to startle guests. That is, until they recline with mojito in hand and gaze out at the ocean.

A fur pillow in Miami is a touch of Barbarella at the beach—and you can't get much better than that.

Instead of a high-tech modern telescope, I went with a vintage original. It has authenticity and character—and still lets you spy on unsuspecting sunbathers below.

Introduce some fearless into the formal. Don't be afraid to take risks and don't take yourself—or your home—too seriously.

Hanging a Robert Moody acrylic in the humid confines of a bathroom isn't usually recommended, but install a freestanding glass shower in front of the artwork, and the problem's solved.

JUST ADD WATER

Yes, that's a glass-enclosed shower right in the middle of this bachelor pad bedroom. It's totally unorthodox, but it transforms the plumbing and the fixtures into freestanding sculpture—and lets him keep tabs on MarketWatch as he suds up, especially important if you're a Manhattan workaholic who only dashes home to shower and sleep.

This primitive stool is just about the last thing you would expect to find in this super-refined, book-lined study—and that's why it works.

DEN OF ANTIQUITIES

In a room with a fireplace, the hearth is usually the focal point. That's why there's practically an unwritten rule that a sofa or chairs have to face the mantelpiece or be positioned at right angles to it. Since I'm not big on decor dictums, I totally disregarded all that for this sophisticated but offbeat grouping. Jettisoning a sofa altogether, I opted instead for two custom velvet-tufted recamier chaises. Ideal for chilling and less visually imposing than a couch, they add graceful elegance along with their unexpectedness. Twin floor lamps with substantial shades are another choreographed quirk. I went with bold lighting rather than something less intrusive because it helps balance the delicacy of the chaises.

To concentrate their visual impact, I grouped the owner's entire collection of Greek and Roman antiquities in a single bookcase instead of scattering them piecemeal throughout the room.

Don't be hyper-respectful of the bathroom. Decorate it like any other room, with upholstered furniture, artwork, and fresh flowers.

In the months when a fire's not lit, an earthy, sculptural arrangement of twigs fills the hearth.

A CLEAN GETAWAY

While it looks like a sophisticated living room, this sumptuous space, *right*, is actually—surprise!—part of the bathroom on the opposite page. The high-gloss hardwood floors, fireplace, framed artwork, upholstered furniture, and leather tote create the feel of a spa retreat and complement the sleek lines of the rolled-lip tub.

This pair of sconces
and the vases
underneath set
off the tub and
draw attention to
its shapely, sinuous
silhouette.

A concrete bowl corrals stacks of
fresh towels tubside, plus the
roughened texture plays off the
smooth shine of the floors.

TIP #9 : Don't let your house boss you around

More times than I can count, I've visited prospective clients who never cook and never entertain yet have a fully decorated, pristine dining room. Maybe it sees action once every few years during the holidays. It's an incredible waste of space that would work so much better with their lifestyle if it could be converted into a home office, library/den, or family/media room. But they almost never make the switch. They'll keep not using the dining room because they're tyrannized by their floor plan. Just because an architect wrote "guest bedroom" on a blueprint back in the day or a contractor pre-installed a dining room chandelier in the middle of the ceiling during construction doesn't mean that's how a space should be used. Hello, news flash: It's *your* home.

Think of all the rooms in your home as open to interpretation. Don't be influenced by how a previous homeowner allocated the space or by a realtor's comments during a walk-through. If you want to turn a master suite into a combo bedroom/playroom for your toddler twins, why shouldn't you? If your living room has panoramic views of your backyard garden, you love to cook and entertain, and you're a horticulture enthusiast, why can't it become your indoor-outdoor kitchen/dining area? And the same goes for how you decide to decorate the room itself. There's no rule that says you can't use a sophisticated table lamp on a kitchen counter or hang prized artwork next to the coffeemaker. Remember: It's all about your lifestyle and the way *you* live. With a little determination and an occasional call to a contractor or handyman, customizing your home is limited only by your imagination.

ON THE WATERFRONT

Since these seaside Miami digs were all about the dazzling ocean vistas, I wasn't going to be bullied by the apartment's architecture and window placement when it came to design. In the bedroom, *above*, I positioned the bed so it directly faced the view of the water and created an efficient room divider in the process. A TV placed in front of the window lets the owner lie in bed, channel surf, and scope out surf breaks at the same time.

A steady stream of visitors is a given with a beachfront apartment. But rather than abdicating a guest bedroom solely to out-of-towners, this study, with its sophisticated version of a daybed, caters to the owner.

> *kitchens can have practicality and panache. Just as long as you bring something else to the table besides cabinetry and appliances.*

A RECIPE FOR STYLE

Because it's such a function-specific zone, the kitchen is usually considered off-limits when it comes to asserting your autonomy. But just because there's a fridge and a stove in there doesn't mean you can't design according to your lifestyle. At my lake house, *opposite*, the best place for the kitchen was—under the stairs. It's a convenient, compact, and cozy spot for meal prep and hanging out. It also freed up floor space for a larger living room, since I'm not known only for my culinary skills ... and I do like to entertain.

Artwork in the kitchen doesn't have to be gastronomically themed. In this South Beach kitchen, a sculpture by abstract expressionist Louise Nevelson is a dramatic, moody departure from the expected and definitely not a watercolor of a bowl of fruit.

The stairs leading to the second floor have become a hangout spot where guests sit on the steps and chat with the designated chef du jour.

Articulated mirrors mounted on either side of the window replace a typical medicine cabinet setup.

SOAP STARS

If you have a spectacular view, optimize it, even if it's in the bathroom. Vanities are often relegated to the largest wall, but that doesn't take advantage of what's outside the window. Placing the sink, *above*, to look out at the cityscape meant the clients could admire the street scene every time they washed up.

Sleek tub and sink
surrounds in minimalist
wood are (in the hands
of a good finisher) more
practical than they
would seem.

TIP #10 : Adding by subtracting

Less is more is one of the most difficult concepts to get across as a designer. Convincing people that sometimes it's better to take away to improve a room is a tough sell—especially when they've hired you to help them buy new stuff. They immediately suspect you're trying to bully them into tossing out all their worldly possessions or that you're creating an exercise in austere design that will leave them with a vacant, stylized

room and a single conceptual chair. What adding by subtracting is really about is editing. You want to be selective about the pieces you have, so each of them is impactful, with forms that function and that make a purposeful statement. These choice objects should have simple lines or a strong emotional connection to who you are and what you're about. And you're already doing it pretty effectively in other areas of your life. Because I'm betting that you don't wear all the clothes in your closet when you go into the office, that you don't display photos of every person you've ever met, and that you don't use all your dishes to serve dinner. You streamline, you curate, you downselect. Apply the same standards to your interiors. Three perfectly shaped, sculptural candlesticks can have more of a design presence than twenty-four not-so-amazing candlesticks. A single enormous canvas can be more eye-catching than a dozen smaller artworks. Remember my K.I.S.S. motto: Keep it simple, stupid. Because I like it simple, and I'm stupid.

SERVING SUGGESTIONS

I'll be honest: A pared-back decor does require some ruthlessness. Lose the clutter, because if your junk is stratifying into geological layers, that's a deal-killer for minimalism. In this dining room, *above*, an imposing mirror substitutes for lots of itty-bitty prints and photos. On the table sit just a few perfectly formed pieces of serving- and drinkware rather than a cacophony.

Artwork echoes the sharp angularity and colors of the surround, ottoman, and geometric rug.

This fireplace surround of black marble was reduced to just the simplest lines. Without a mantel, there's no place for tchotchkes to accumulate.

Create drama with bold shifts in scale. This massive, openwork light fixture plays off the diminutive size of the gold sphere vase.

An expansive sweep of wall is broken up by only a single black-framed painting by Matisse—did I just say that?—with a power belying its size.

AS GOOD AS IT GETS

When a room features only a few pieces, each of them has to be stellar, with strong shapes and distinctive style, like this 1950s saddle-stitched armchair, *opposite*, and lacquered X-table in a Manhattan apartment. A slope-armed lounger, *above*, is unfussy and elegant, and a vase with an intricate black-and-white design is the only pattern in the room.

Two strongly related objects can sometimes have more impact than one larger piece, especially when they're as sleek and organic as these almost identical vases.

MAKING AN ENTRANCE

Entryway consoles, which are prime dropping-off spots for mail, keys, homework, and magazines, can easily turn into junk-o-ramas. Keep yours looking pristine by creating a tableau that discourages piling on. Lamps of concentric circles, *below*, stand sentrylike on either side of abstract artwork. In between, a well-considered mix of pottery references the colors of the print and shapes of the lights. Note that all of the pots are lower than the edge of the print, so there's no visual interference between them, and that all of them are decorative—so no dumping stuff inside.

Mounting a bedside lamp on the wall near the headboard frees up space on a nightstand for a simple grouping of pottery and plant.

Drawers are a necessity for camouflaging clutter. Shut them, and your TV remote and BlackBerry disappear, at least until morning.

Mood #1 ORGANIC

Green design's appeal is obvious. Products and materials that are sustainable, renewable, and earth-friendly help preserve the planet's dwindling resources and show respect for the interconnectedness of everything and everyone living on it. Organic objects also have one-of-a-kind beauty that acknowledges the perfection in imperfection. Think of a divider screen crafted from rough-hewn slabs of a downed sycamore tree with all of its unique knots and grain patterns. Or a handblown, recycled-glass wine jug, just slightly asymmetrical, that becomes a unique lamp. Or a window shade hand-woven from sun-bleached grasses. Organic design is also about what's appropriate. It means asking what makes sense in terms of the environment, the location, the architecture—and your own personal narrative. An East Coast beach cottage decorated as if it were a desert hacienda just doesn't feel right. But introduce references to the nearby saltwater and dunes, and it suddenly seems balanced and attuned to its surroundings. The same goes for interiors that aren't reflective of who you really are and the way you really live—they seem forced, false, and inauthentic. But the opposite will happen when rooms are in sync with your personality. They click, as if they effortlessly fell into place. You feel at home. Because staying true to yourself is the ultimate expression of organic design.

BOTH GOOD FOR THE EARTH AND GOOD-LOOKING, THESE RESPONSIBLY CRAFTED EXTRAS ARE AS STYLISH AS THEY ARE SUSTAINABLE

1. Shades woven from natural fibers are a smart way to finish your windows and soften the world beyond.

2. With a base made from a repurposed vintage wine bottle and a shade of all-natural twine, this **eco-chic lamp** is an easy, stylish way to light up your life.

3. Constructed from recycled glass and reclaimed cerused oak, these **Oneida side tables** I designed combine refinement and environmental sensitivity.

4. Thanks to an abaca rug, wooded forest wall covering, and grass patterned textiles, this **all-natural, organically inspired palette** creates a clean, fresh look and feel that brings the outdoors in.

NATURE'S CALLING

To make the organic orgasmic, opt for rich, natural textures layered with a sophisticated hand, like Michelle Oka Doner's bronze sculpture, *Burning Bush*.

Mood #2 REFINED

Everyone loves design's "wow!" moments. But quiet can speak volumes, too. These soft-spoken elements are what I call refined. They signal an appreciation of the understated and the elegant. Refinement is really about clarity of vision. It's about sublime lines and hushed tones. Some of the best examples of refined design are antiques, but newly made pieces inspired by historical styles can be equally sophisticated. The refinement happens in the editing, with ornamental flourishes and decorative touches toned down and muted. Like a painted Swedish settee upholstered in oatmeal-colored linen and silk. Or a pair of Italian Savonarola-styled armchairs covered in cut velvet and suede. Or a simple but elegant set of sterling-silver julep cups used for your favorite cocktail or as timeless vases. Refinement is in the details, in pieces that are perfectly polished and exquisitely formed. Choose elements that support your style without overpowering it. Use them casually and confidently to express the pleasures of living well—and don't save them only for a special occasion. Eat Chinese takeout—along with breakfast, lunch, and dinner—with sterling-silver flatware, if you're lucky enough to have it. Dress your bed with the highest thread count cotton sheets you can afford and finish with a beautiful bedspread or coverlet that expresses your

GOOD-BYE CRASS, HELLO CLASS—THESE POSH TOUCHES LEND UPPER-CRUST PANACHE TO ANY INTERIOR

1. Silver-plated **cocktail accoutrements**, from equestrian bottle openers to shakers to julep cups, are a cosmopolitan way to raise the bar on mixology style.

2. Two 1940s **Italian chairs** covered in zigzagging cut velvet and suede are urbane additions to a style- and decades-spanning room.

3. With their luxurious feel and hushed tones, these **misty, quiet fabrics** speak refinement loud and clear.

4. Gavin Ziegler's sleek-and-chic **abstract bronze sculpture** is a distinctive way to bring art into an interior without nailing it to the wall.

5. Based on an enduring Egyptian design that dates back to the time of the pharaohs, my oak **French Fort bench** features curvaceous, classic lines.

HIGH STYLE

A subtle collection of artwork, furnishings, and accessories—not matched but coordinated—sets a tone of understated refinement.

Mood #3 SEXY

There's sensuality in good design. Decorating is about suggestion. It's about what you see when you walk into a room … and what you don't. It's about creating visual tension, charging a space with subtle electricity, and making guests wonder what will come next. To achieve this slow reveal, use textures and materials that have a subdued eroticism. Metallic foil wallpaper with shimmer, mirrored consoles, a waterfall chandelier, slightly smoky antiqued mirrors, and leather tiles all hint at decadence. Engage all the senses to create ambiance. Furniture should make you want to sink into it and recline. Fragrance, like an aromatic scented candle or a reed diffuser, and evocative music, like a CD by an obscure jazz musician you first heard at an out-of-the-way nightclub, all add mystery. Lighting that directs the gaze to strategic places adds to the drama and anticipation. Flickering candlelight that casts shadows, indirect illumination that gives off a soft glow, and a dimmer that approximates dusk are must-haves. Sexiness is also created by intimacy, so form secluded conversation spots and nooks away from high-traffic zones. Try a pair of wing chairs and a sized-for-two dining table in the quiet corner of a great room or a small sofa or daybed and a pair of accent tables on a large stair landing. Let people share unguarded moments and make connections, which is what sexy design is all about.

LET YOUR ROOM
SLIP INTO
SOMETHING A
LITTLE FLIRTATIOUS
WITH EXTRAS THAT
TEMPT, TEASE, AND
TANTALIZE

1. An intimate **lounge area** within the living room feels private and personal.

2. Nestled in a wood-and-leather holder, this **aromatic scented candle** looks as come-hither as it smells.

3. A hammered-copper, low-slung **suede-on-suede chair** has a seductive stance and alluring materials.

4. Slipped over a naked Edison light bulb, a **wire mesh shade** becomes lingerie for your lighting.

5. The tufted leather and ebonized bamboo of my custom **Bash Bish bench** creates sexy, modern lines.

6. A sophisticated and masculine **mixing of fabrics and materials** forms a sultry foundation for any room.

SOAK IT UP

This luxuriously appointed bath reflects a strong sense of elegance and relaxed sophistication. The focal point of the room, the French-style, hand-hammered copper bathtub rests sculpture-like on a rosewood slab and is lit by a steel candelabra floor lamp. It's an artful, surprising, imaginative blend that instantly conveys comfort—and sexiness.

Mood #4 PURE

People want to come home to a sanctuary, a soothing respite from all the stresses and anxieties of the outside world. They want honesty of form, design that reflects pride in craftsmanship and doesn't try to be something that it's not. It should be the calm amidst the chaos, steeped in quiet and pared down to its essence. Pure pieces are timeless and reliable and anti-extravagant, the decorating equivalent of your favorite pair of blue jeans and a crisp white linen shirt. My favorites are textural abaca rugs, bars of all-natural vegetable soap, unglazed pottery, recycled-glass dinner plates, natural string lampshades, and paintings without frames. Pure is classic and clean-lined and doesn't jar the eye with harsh hues or extraneous details. This Zen-like tranquility starts with clearing away clutter, removing the excess and the unwanted and the inessential. What remains should be elemental and functional and all-the-time beautiful. Luxurious cashmere throws. Unfinished steel-edge mirrors. Black-and-white photography. It's effortless décor that never feels dated and always looks fresh.

SOUL-SATISFYING AND SERENE, THESE DESIGNS CAPTURE THE ESSENCE OF THE OBJECT

1. A **recycled-glass bowl** filled with all-natural, ramie-fiber washcloths and dye-free organic soaps is a thoughtful luxury.

2. Designed by Piero Lissoni, the **lacquered Classica chair** is precise and minimal and epitomizes pure design.

3. My custom **Tully tables**, crafted from etched slate and recycled metal, have a purity of line and material.

4. Roberto Dutesco's **photographs** of the wild horses on Nova Scotia's Sable Island are awe-inspiring and transporting.

5. A classic since they were introduced in 1956, **Eero Saarinen's iconic tables** have a clarity and crispness that's utterly timeless.

ROOM WITH A VIEW

The perfect recipe for pure design effortlessly combines simplicity, beauty—and the one-of-a-kind handiwork of Mother Nature.

Mood #5 WARM

Imagine coming home on a snowy winter evening and curling up in front of a crackling fire with a mug of hot chocolate, a snuggly throw, and a dozing dog at your feet. That safe, cozy feeling is what warm interiors are all about. They're familiar and unpretentious, and grounded, and reassuring, no matter the season—or the style. An urban loft can achieve this comfy-ness every bit as much as a mountain cabin filled with wool plaids, stone hearths, and Labrador retrievers. Homey, low-maintenance fabrics, sturdy furniture, salvaged woods, and lighting that creates a soft glow connect us to a sense of being cared for. Open, free-flowing floor plans that don't shut off rooms or family members encourage together time and conversation. Deep-pile wool carpets, a bed with a collection of inviting down pillows and a delicious duvet, and a stack of well-read and well-thumbed books and magazines can beckon and soothe.

COZY UP TO HOMEY ACCESSORIES AND FURNITURE THAT ARE THE DECORATING EQUIVALENT OF COMFORT FOOD

1. Plush velvet pillows and a down-filled bolster coddle and delight.
2. Whether it's the familiar crackling of a fireplace or shadow-casting candlelight, **flickering flames** create ambience with a strong emotional connection.
3. My classically inspired, clean-lined **Saratoga sofa** embraces you with its sink-into-it comfort and exaggerated length.
4. Piles of books, from best sellers to children's classics, are must-haves when you want to hunker down and chill out.
5. Luxurious blankets and throws are snuggling essentials.
6. Sumptuous sensations underfoot are the true foundation of warm interiors.

DOWN TIME

The mix of light and dark woods, the gentle glow of lamplight, and the multiple layers and textures of materials create a sophisticated, cocoonlike setting around my custom-designed Manlius sofa.

Mood #6 BALANCED

Rooms feel best when they're in a state of equilibrium. All the opposing influences—subtle and over-the-top, rarefied and everyday, genteel and raucous, racy and prim—harmonize with each other, creating a style that doesn't veer too much in one direction or another. The challenge (and the fun) in decorating is achieving this state of congruousness. Lots of times people confuse balance with symmetry. Balance is about calibrating all of a room's components, from the furniture layout to the color palette to the floor coverings, fabrics, and finishes, so that no one style has more—or less—visual impact. It's rough-cut fireplace wood stored next to the hearth in a sleek and modern Pyrex glass container. It's $5 Crate and Barrel tumblers mixed in with your favorite Baccarat. It's an antique Japanese screen next to your Jean-Michel Frank–style sofa that costs $1,200 (including delivery). It's light and dark, thick and thin, matte and shiny, weighty and weightless. When you're able to achieve this level of balanced contradictions, your space feels comfortable and in control, like driving a car when its wheels are properly aligned. With each element in proportion to the next, you've achieved an interior that looks—and lives—just right.

THROW A ROOM A CURVEBALL BY COMBINING DISPARATE STYLES AND CENTURIES—JUST MAKE SURE IT'S ALL IN EQUILIBRIUM

1. This room is aligned not only in its textures, finishes, and materials but also in its **strong use of symmetry**.

2. A minimalist, machine-polished **glass ice bucket** finds its perfect counterpart in organic, branch-style ice tongs.

3. My custom **Drumlins dining table** is a balancing act of three materials: a steel base, a charcoal-hued paperstone top, and a bamboo inlay.

4. The juxtaposition of naturally shed **vintage antlers** mounted on a modern Lucite plaque showcases two opposing yet complementary elements.

5. Create a **striking tablescape** with a pleasing visual tension. Start with a refined linen place mat and a simple cotton napkin, then layer on sterling-silver flatware, a sophisticated Hermès salad dish, a basic white dinner plate, and an affordable, roughly finished Japanese bowl.

BALANCING ACT

The coupling of asymmetry (the items on the table) with symmetry (the two flanking trees) establishes the room's cohesive feel.

Mood #7 FUN

Interiors shouldn't take themselves too seriously. Cheekiness and playfulness are disarming and help put people at ease. Unstuffy pieces bring levity to a space, changing the staid and static into the lively and energetic. Photos of friends and relatives being the life of the party, artwork done by the kids and displayed front and center, over-the-top wallpaper patterned with ironic illustrations, a carved-wood deer head—all are easygoing touches that show your house is a home, not an uptight museum. Quirky colors and whimsical patterns, especially when they're used unexpectedly and creatively, can loosen up a too-formal space. A Parsons-style table painted citrus orange, a vintage chair upholstered in electric-blue vinyl, a painting depicting a big pink dog all jolt a room with subversiveness and winking wit. Humorous design feels light and airy and a little out-there. It takes risks, makes its own rules, shakes things up. Nothing is off-limits or out of bounds. A fun-loving room always passes the Twister test: there's nothing so precious about it that you'd be afraid to unroll a multicolored plastic mat, spin a dial, and contort yourself on the floor as a human game piece.

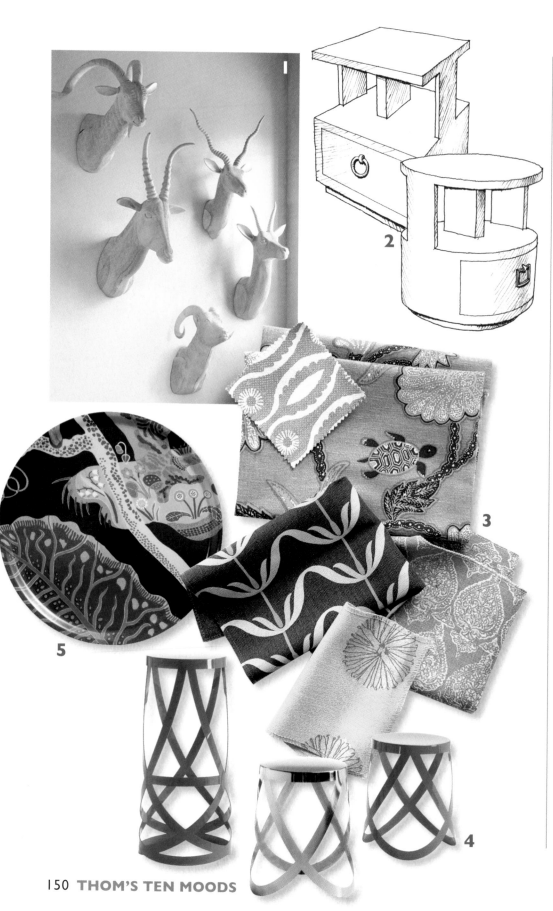

GET THE PARTY STARTED—EVEN IF YOU'RE NOT ENTERTAINING—WITH IRREVERENT DESIGNS THAT ARE CAUSE FOR CELEBRATION

1. Trophy heads of reedbucks, blesboks, bighorn sheep, and catalina goats, all hand-carved from basswood, put a whimsical spin on stodgy taxidermy.

2. My custom **Sedgwick bedside tables**, which come in a variety of colors and finishes and feature stylized cutouts, bring unstuffy design to any space.

3. High-contrast colors and cheeky patterns—turtles, abstract florals worthy of Dr. Seuss—give these textiles a zany liveliness.

4. For insta-fun, try these **cartoon-bright stools** with laser-cut metal that loops and swirls like curling ribbon.

5. Serve up something wacky with a **melamine tray** featuring the trippy patterns of Swedish designer Josef Franks.

HUMOR ME

Fun is all about using fresh, youthful, and bold elements fearlessly. Here, a restrained, modern interior suddenly comes alive with a just-picked palm frond, a Lucite box atop a graphic Capron-tile table, and a vivid striped pillow.

Mood #8 INVITING

In a welcoming home where no RSVP is required, nothing is off-limits or precious. You can relax on the couch with a glass of red wine, eat off the fine china without needing a special occasion, help yourself to whatever's in the well-stocked fridge. Thoughtful choices and generosity create spaces that are so hospitable friends and family will instantly know that you delight in their company. Put comfort first. Select furnishings for their ergonomics and their usability. Choose beautiful, comfortable dining chairs rather than delicate antiques or modern sculptural versions, stain-hiding slipcovers in dark colors instead of white silk upholstery, a deep nap-worthy sofa with plenty of pillows over a stiff, tight-backed couch. Interiors that are gracious and forgiving, that can handle mishaps like spilled drinks or drooling babies or muddy paws, are the ones people want to return to. If pieces are too fragile and too precious, visitors will be inhibited. Make them feel at ease with surfaces that don't require coasters and upholstery that can handle life's spills. Pay attention to the small gesture. A clearly visible house number, stacks of fluffy guest towels and a terry cloth robe, backgammon sets and decks of cards for impromptu games, kid-friendly snacks stocked in the pantry, extra dog leashes, and a round dining table that can squeeze in just one more—all show you think about what's often overlooked. Which is the very definition of inviting.

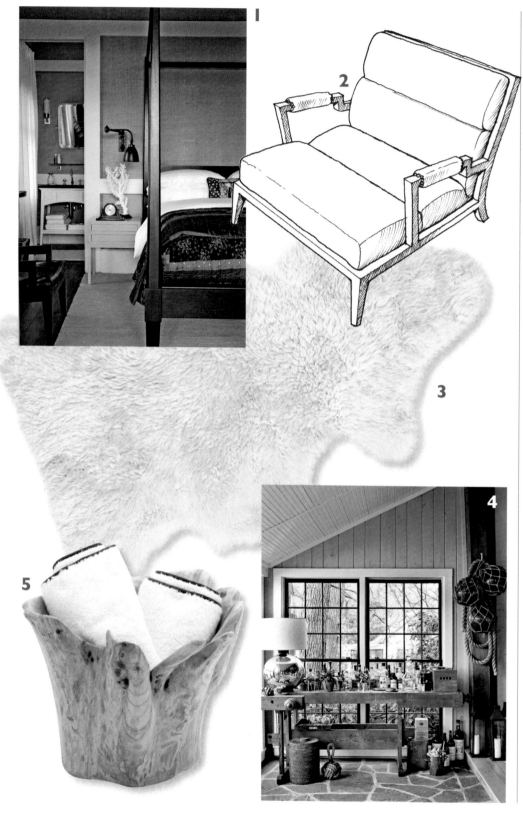

WELCOMING, STAY-AWHILE EXTRAS MAKE GUESTS FEEL AT HOME AND TURN EVERY DAY INTO A SPECIAL OCCASION

1. Guest **bedroom must-haves:** a bed layered with high-quality sheets, pillows, and blankets, a well-lit bathroom, and a nightstand within arm's reach. Just don't be surprised if your visitors start forwarding their mail—to your address.

2. The best seat in the house? This custom **Armory Square lounger** with comfy padded arms and generous cushions that I designed using ebonized bamboo.

3. Nothing's as beckoning as a **fluffy, supersoft sheepskin.** Toss these snowy pelts over ottomans, chairs, even the foot of a bed for a quick hit of comfort.

4. Be ready for impromptu entertaining with a **fully stocked, all-access bar** that serves up top-shelf style along with cocktails.

5. Pamper guests—and yourself—with luxurious, **ultra-absorbent bath sheets** that turn an ordinary shower into a spa-worthy indulgence.

CREATURE COMFORTS

Inviting interiors can also extend to the outdoors. A lakeside deck kitted out with a fire pit, candles, cozy wicker chairs, and a pillow-heaped daybed encourages into-the-evening lingering.

Mood #9 EXOTIC

Silk pillows sewn from an antique Japanese kimono. A hammered silver tray from India. Beautifully glazed, unusual ceramics from around the world—or pieces that look like they are. Vibrant-colored, flat weave Turkish kilim. What's unfamiliar and foreign can invigorate a room, introducing a sense of the faraway. The juxtaposition of cultures creates and heightens contrasts, transforming what's ordinary in a distant country into the extraordinary here. Elements from remote locales connect us to the global community, reminding us that style transcends borders and time zones. Exotic isn't always literal. An international-inspired interior can be subtle, with the feel of a particular place reinterpreted and distilled, so the ethnic essence remains. A klismos dining chair, with its splayed legs and curved back, looks clean-lined but doesn't shout its Hellenic Greek origins. A two-toned batik pillow with a fun color palette and abstract pattern looks totally current but is based on an antique fabric. Small touches brought back from your travels or pieces that evoke an unforgettable trip, like a Moroccan leather hassock, Russian icon, teak sculpture from Bali, or lacquered box from Indonesia, serve as reminders of the connectedness of cultures. Because homes need an inkling of where we've been and what's inspired us along life's travels.

IT TAKES A GLOBAL VILLAGE TO DECORATE A HOME, SO BE ADVENTUROUS WITH THESE FAR-FLUNG FINDS—AND LEAVE YOUR PASSPORT BEHIND

1. Candy for the eyes and the intellect, these **graphic textiles** showcase traditional patterns from India, Japan, and Spain.

2. There's a discreet ethnicity to these **textural stools**, which are a sophisticated comingling of South American macan wood and pita fiber.

3. A trio of **serving plates** with international origins— hand-hammered Indian silver, Moroccan back-painted glass, and raku-fired glazed porcelain from Japan—are small but speak with noticeable accents.

4. Well-traveled **vintage rugs** can introduce some cross-cultural flair to a space.

5. Hand-screened ikat pillows combine a centuries-old pattern with a fresh and modern color palette.

6. The leather-strap seat and formfitting back of my **Greek Peak chair** captures the spirit of ancient Athens in a timely fashion— think of it as contemporary stand-in for the fifth-century-B.C. original.

FOREIGN AFFAIRS

From the faux African ivory tusks to the Italian leather stools to the Afghani rug to everything in between, this wide-ranging room is a veritable United Nations of decor.

YOUR MOOD HERE

vibrant EDGY glamorous
tranquil SPICY cheeky
charming TIMELESS
timely HONEST tantalizing
PROVOCATIVE dynamic
MEDITATIVE electrifying
SNAPPY uplifting
SASSY individualistic

Since I'm all about personalized design, this last mood is up to you. Choose one (or more) from this list, or come up with your own.

ECCENTRIC regal NOSTALGIC
CITIFIED lavish WHIMSICAL
cultural OFFBEAT seductive
URBANE demure
UNCOMPLICATED strong
ENCHANTING playful
WITTY irreverent
FRESH serene

PULLING IT ALL TOGETHER

Now that you're familiar with my ten moods and my ten tips, I'm going to show you some standout examples of what happens when you combine them. And as you'll see, according to my decorating arithmetic, one plus one equals a lot more than two.

In this Manhattan showhouse, *below*, I indulged in rarefied objects, like handcrafted wood-pulp wallpaper, English pewter boxes, and an antique projector mirror. Which is why I added the statement-making, plaster-look eagle console. It's a bold gesture that invigorates the space while preserving its sophisticated style. A beach-house sun room, *right*, has a casual, spontaneous feel: there's a pair of tufted-back striped lounge chairs, a vintage marble-topped coffee table, galvanized-metal porch lights used as sconces, and a no-fuss abaca rug. It's a low-maintenance mix that's practically an invitation to prop up bare feet.

INVITING +
There's truth in texture

REFINED +
Every room needs a surprise

Rooted in tradition but totally of the moment, this eagle-shaped console I designed updates an all-American emblem.

These ceramic feel-good fakes resemble gargantuan clam shells but don't harm the ocean's fragile ecosystem.

Instead of the obligatory dozen red roses, try less-expected flora with unusual shapes and scents.

SEXY +
Color your world (sort of)

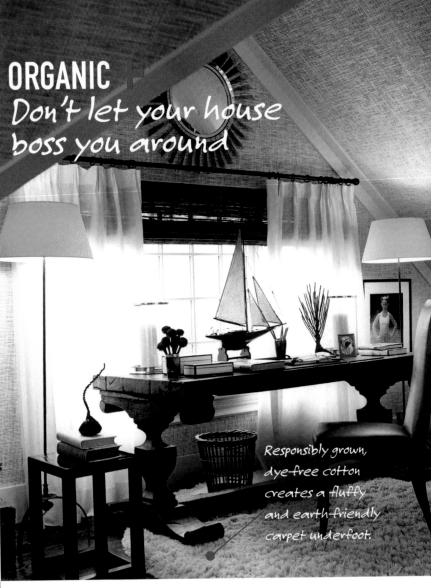

ORGANIC
Don't let your house boss you around

Responsibly grown, dye-free cotton creates a fluffy and earth-friendly carpet underfoot.

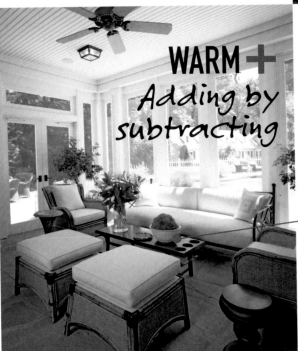

WARM +
Adding by subtracting

Glam, shimmery surfaces and blooming flora have an inherent seductiveness. A golden-hued vase, *above left*, brimming with red-orange pincushion protea, plays up the yellow edging on a lacquered accent table. This low-ceilinged dormer, *above right*, is an unexpectedly accommodating spot for a substantial antique Irish hall table repurposed as a desk. A poolside solarium, *left*, is pared down and uncluttered but still stay-awhile-comfy, thanks to the generously cushioned daybed and angle-backed rattan and bamboo chairs.

A simple stoneware bowl heaped with moss is a chic, minimalist alternative to a meticulously arranged bouquet.

ORGANIC +
Truth in texture

Statement-making pendant lamps, box overheads, and overscaled pillar candles, *below*, offer a variety of illumination options in a sleek-meets-sophisticated kitchen. Nestled in a woven-rope basket and surrounded by moss, two spare Japanese plants, *right*, introduce some greenery and natural forms to a tableau of klismos chairs and framed black-and-white photos. Humble factory gears are elevated to artwork, *bottom right*, when displayed on stands and grouped in a trio atop an elegant marble coffee table.

BALANCED +
Light up your life

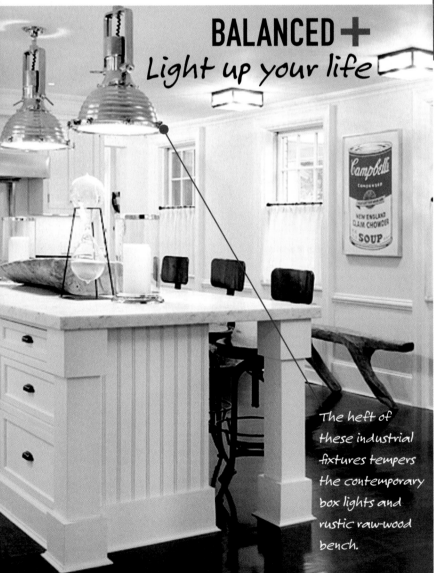

The heft of these industrial fixtures tempers the contemporary box lights and rustic raw-wood bench.

FUN +
Lose the matchy-matchiness

EXOTIC +
Clashing is dashing

Canopied wing chairs are as cozy as they are stately.

REFINED +
Lay out a plan

A weathered cast-iron cannonball from Puerto Rico, *top left*, references the client's nationality and sits companionably beside family photos in sterling-silver frames. Circular dining tables like this one, *above*, are friendlier—you can always squeeze in just one more guest, and there's no one presiding at the head of the table. Cedar shingles, installed in a small Hamptons beach-house bedroom, *bottom left*, are a subversive nod to the area's most common building material.

FUN +
The smaller the space, the bigger the risk

Silk-screened bug pillows are a playful entomological reference to a summer home's inevitable creepy-crawlies.

Part II CASE STUDIES

I promised you that by the book's end you'd be sufficiently prepped to decorate solo, and we're almost there. At this point, you're well versed in my accessible-to-all design philosophy. You have an appreciation for how moods can give a space edge and energy. You're in possession of my top-notch, fail-safe decorating tips. And you've started to learn how to pull all this know-how together in concrete and eye-catching ways. The only missing component is applying everything you just learned to an entire room, house, or apartment in a way that makes sense for you and your lifestyle. That's what we're about to embark on now. In the following pages I'll guide you through five highly personal interiors geared to homeowners with unique needs. I explain the how and why of each decorating decision, and do it in a way that will allow you to apply the principles to your abode. First is an urban loft for a hip young couple who wanted a chic, art-filled space that would adapt easily when they started a family. Second is a dreamy bedroom for a courageous, fun-loving mother of two who wanted a versatile boudoir that could function as both a tranquil private sanctuary and an inviting hangout spot with her kids. Third is an example from *Dress My Nest* that details how fashion and some personal items can be amazing jumping-off points for interior style. Fourth is all about eco-decorating like you've never seen it before—sexy, luxurious rooms in one of the greenest residential buildings ever constructed. And our national contest winner, whose family room is finally, finally ready for its close-up. Ready to get going? Then read on, and let me show you how to put the *fun* in functional

Case Study #1 AND BABY MAKES THREE

Like a lot of first-time parents, this couple faced an all-too-common design dilemma: how to create interiors that are kid-friendly but still adult sophisticated. Their inviting apartment is a lesson in ingenuity, practicality, and easygoing elegance.

Think of it as the loft that wasn't but is now. When my clients and I first looked at this 2,000-square-foot space, the building was in the process of converting from a live/work structure to a residential co-op. So what did I see? Basically, just a big mess. There were a few makeshift plywood partitions but no proper walls (and therefore no rooms to speak of), a toilet, window air conditioners, and warped and buckled floors that were falling apart. The place was not, repeat, *not* an apartment: it was a floor-through hazard zone with lots of light, great views, and fabulous potential.

First I came up with a layout, one that kept the loftlike quality of the original interior but served the needs of two young New York professionals who like to spend time with their friends, who entertain, and who plan on eventually having kids. I wanted to leave as much open space as open as possible but create private areas without putting up too many walls—tricky. The two entrances (an elevator that opens directly into the loft and a back door in what's now the laundry room), the placement of the windows, the structural columns, and the wet wall (that's existing plumbing) created logical parameters for how to organize the interior organically into living, dining, and sleeping spaces, plus kitchen, bath, and laundry.

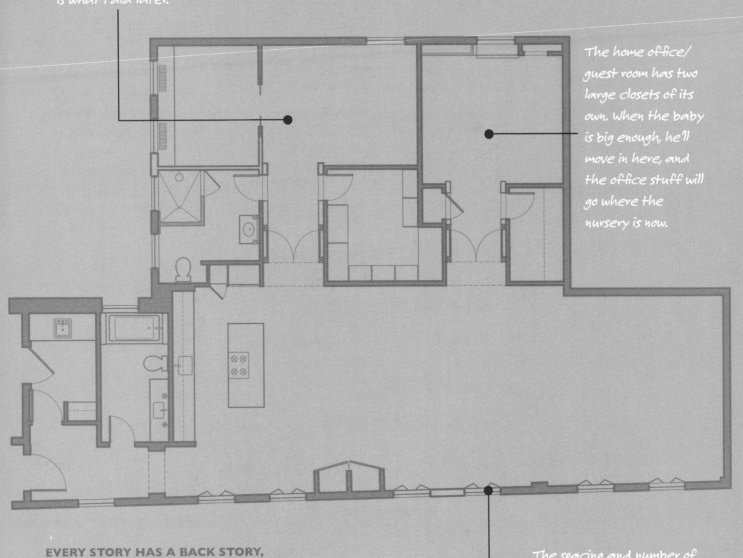

Floor plans not only organize space, they can create flexibility for the future. The master bedroom suite is large enough to partition off an area for a nursery, which is what I did later.

The home office/ guest room has two large closets of its own. When the baby is big enough, he'll move in here, and the office stuff will go where the nursery is now.

EVERY STORY HAS A BACK STORY, AND IN DESIGN IT'S THE FLOOR PLAN

Design is all about internal logic, about organizing a place so that it makes sense for how and where we live. Here, structural columns and windows suggested an organic way to divide the interior into "rooms" without building lots of unloftlike walls. Relationships are key, and function is central: kitchen, dining, and living spaces flow naturally into one another; master bedroom and home office/guest bedroom are adjacent and entered via similar pocket doors; laundry and mud rooms share the wet wall with the kitchen, powder room, and master bath.

The spacing and number of windows made dividing the open space into kitchen, dining, and living areas easy: each has two windows.

To make an architecturally seamless change, I used two retractable doors to close off the nursery from the master bedroom. Thanks to windows on two walls, each space has lots of light.

Why not include beautiful warm elements in the guest bathroom, laundry room, and vestibule? Here the powder room doubles as a guest bathroom for visiting friends.

Let's face it: today's kitchen is a part of the living room, so the white surfaces and open shelves needed to blend right into the architecture.

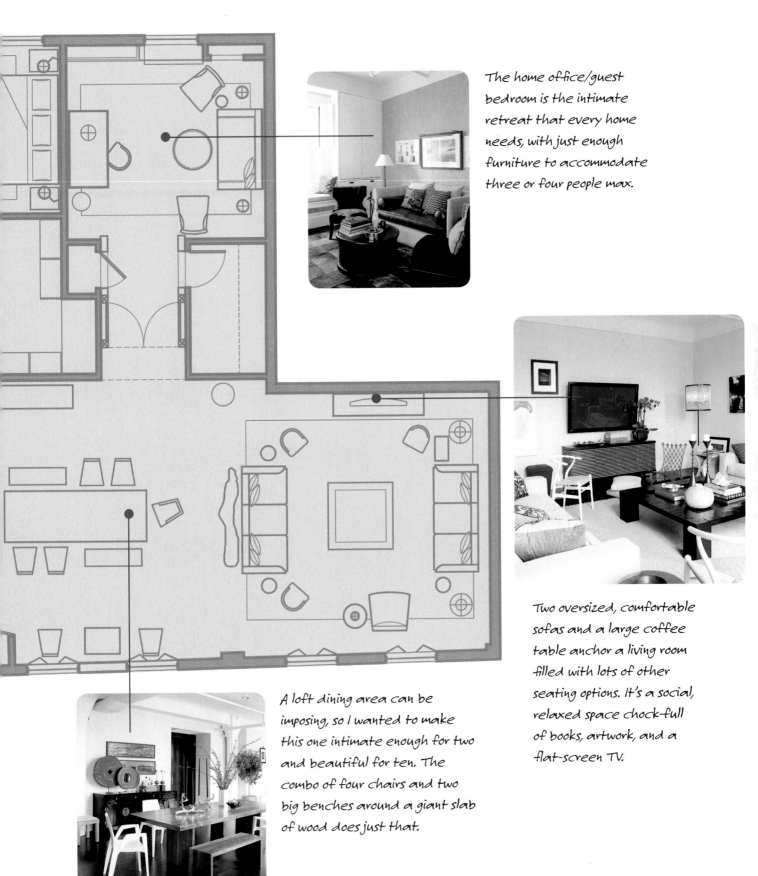

The home office/guest bedroom is the intimate retreat that every home needs, with just enough furniture to accommodate three or four people max.

Two oversized, comfortable sofas and a large coffee table anchor a living room filled with lots of other seating options. It's a social, relaxed space chock-full of books, artwork, and a flat-screen TV.

A loft dining area can be imposing, so I wanted to make this one intimate enough for two and beautiful for ten. The combo of four chairs and two big benches around a giant slab of wood does just that.

Every apartment I do has a signature color; here it's red. The woven-rope chair adds a red-hot moment, and it's a really eye-catching piece of sculpture.

DESIGN IS A BALANCING ACT, AND IT'S SPECIFIC TO YOU

Classic symmetry (paired lamps and sofas) clearly sets the boundaries for a comfortable, approachable, and very stylish living room. A simple, versatile rug edged in chocolate brown is adaptable to any future styles. End tables deliberately don't match: one's a repurposed tractor blade, the other's covered in parchment. While the palette may be neutral (yes, with red splashes), the mix of patterns, textures, and materials (bamboo, parchment, rope, metals, crystal, silver, rush) is anything but. Artwork propped against the wall is bohemian chic, and the piece over the sofa provides the space with a real conclusion.

Art and accessories finish the space and introduce depth, soul, and personality. Depending on the cushions, classic sofas can go in any style direction. These are covered in soft and easy-to-clean Ultrasuede.

This substantial bamboo coffee table displays favorite books and unprecious pottery and is the focal point of the room. The surface is large enough to accommodate kids' games and casual, sit on-the-carpet suppers, and the dark stain echoes the color of the hardwood floors.

When you start with a blank slate of a space, anything's possible. That can be a little scary, so it helps if you're clear about what you need—and what's important to you. I wanted to be sure that the newly designed apartment remained true to its origins as a loft, that it included some elements reflective of the period when the building went up, and that it retained that loftlike sense of wide-open space even though I was adding walls for privacy. I also wanted to make it inviting and warm, fun and comfortable, and full of the clients' personalities.

I decided to leave some traces of the loft's original raw edges exposed, such as the sprinklers, ducts, HVAC system, and structural columns, as reminders that this space had a true industrial past. But I hid some things, too: double closets near the kitchen containing back-of-house stuff like meters and electrical panels were a handy, attractive solution. The kitchen, dining area, and living areas flow naturally from one to the next, with boundaries defined only by furnishings and rugs. Each "room" takes up pretty much the same amount of floor space, as do the transitions in between; an equal distribution of windows (all replaced) along the long wall and the location of the interior columns helped me figure out how to divide the large space naturally.

Double pocket doors separate the master bedroom and home office/guest bedroom from the rest of the interior. When the owners are in bed or in the home office and the doors are open, they can look straight through to the heart of the space. Throughout the loft I've layered lots of patterns, textures, and especially materials. Some, like the subway tiles in the powder room, refer to the building's original era. Others, like the stainless-steel-finished kitchen appliances and eco-friendly cork flooring in the guest bath, are totally today. As for the color palette, it's all about the natural neutrals with splashes of spice.

WHEN IT COMES TO COMFORT, BALANCE IS EVERYTHING

Opposites attract, in design and everything else. For an elegant, comfortable, welcoming room, try a palette of ebony and ivory and build from there, as I did here. The furnishings have elemental forms, classic geometries, clear profiles, and silhouettes that aren't showy or overdesigned. I've contrasted convex and concave curves, circles and squares and rectangles, thick and thin elements, open and closed backs and bases.

The wire horse is fabulous, and the scale is just right for the loft. It marks the transition between the dining and living rooms and adds an organic reference in an industrial way.

White-painted Scandinavian chairs add seating options and new materials into the mix, as do the ceramic side tables flanking the sofa.

A VESTIBULE SHOULD ALWAYS SAY "WELCOME HOME"

Since the elevator door opens directly into the loft, I wanted to create a proper entry that foreshadows what's to come. So I balanced the classic with the eclectic and included organic, fun, and refined elements—from a witty coat tree with branch-shaped hooks to a traditional Turkish rug to a Pyrex umbrella stand that also corrals tennis racquets. Espresso-colored walls and floors showcase the boldly patterned rug. These elements create a comfortable place to take off shoes and add interest to what would otherwise be just a niche for umbrellas. Every foyer should have places for things: somewhere to hang coats and bags, a table with a bowl for keys, a spot for shoes. The ceramic side table is an interesting take on the traditional console—and another material in the mix. Shutters are a great way to control light and privacy; you can always add curtains if you want another layer. The red doors pop, and the color connects everything. I love the little moments and the extra pieces.

BENJAMIN MOORE DEEP ROSE

This vintage lacquered Chinese sideboard not only stores linen and flatware, it also doubles as a bar and a serving piece—and complements the wood slab of the dining table beautifully.

The seating arrangement around the table is deliberate: the chairs are positioned so that when it's just two for dinner, they sit close. The acrylic dining chairs are fun, good-looking, and stackable.

If the goal is to use a room for a variety of purposes, it should be able to accommodate all the activities effortlessly.

The more efficient you are, the more you can enjoy your time at home. This streamlined setup is designed to be stylish as well as create a productive workspace.

Wall coverings made of woven materials bring yet another layer of texture to a room, and help make spaces feel warm and intimate.

THE HOME OFFICE IS A GREAT EXTRA BEDROOM WHEN NEEDED

More intimate than the rest of the loft, the home office serves lots of different purposes. It's a great place to read or hang out with a few friends or just escape for a bit. The palette's darker than the rest of the loft and warm enough to welcome guests when they stay. There's enough space between the desk and the pullout sofabed so that conversions are easy, and the lamps come in handy.

Whether this room happens to function as a home office, library, den, or guest room, great reading lights are important.

Multifunctional, easy-to-move pieces like the coffee and side tables sit on a rug made of natural hides.

Have fun with texture, pattern, and color. Mix them the same way you do with your clothes.

A LITTLE CONTRAST GOES A LONG WAY

Soft, inviting, serene solids provide a great foundation for most rooms. Pale blue, ecru, and lavender, for instance, create an air of tranquility. To add visual texture and a few pops of the unexpected, layer in a fun, refreshing print. If you do, make sure the pattern includes some colors that match your solids (so that everything connects seamlessly) and also complementary hues for contrast and depth. A natural, organic woven blind at the window softens the light and the architecture of the window frame and the wall plane. On the floor, a graphic pattern atop a sober solid such as rich chocolate brown adds a bold, surprising touch.

Bedrooms are meant for relaxing, even though you still have to get up and get out of Dodge every day. Serene blue walls, photographs, and artwork help make this one a refuge.

Layering a rug on top of hard-surface flooring or wall-to-wall carpeting is a great way to bring fresh pattern and color to something plain.

Why not do something different in the nursery? Try a palette of hushed, inviting neutrals and add personality over time with toys and accessories.

BABY-SOFT AND EASY ON THE EYES

In a nursery, safety and function come first. But as far as color goes, you don't have to think just pink or blue anymore. Whether or not you know the gender of your child when you're decorating this sweetest of rooms, there are other options besides the obvious. A gender-free palette is adaptable. It grows with your child over time, and you can add the florals (pink or blue) or the footballs (likewise) later. Start with the basics: soft tones in organic, all-natural, gentle-to-the-touch materials. Stripes are a stylish, visually stimulating choice. Remember: once the bambino arrives, it'll be showered with things that bring gender specificity to the design.

In a nursery, make sure there's night lighting and plenty of storage. I didn't know the baby's gender when I designed the room, so I used striped wallpaper.

I'm a fan of open storage because you can keep everything that you love to see and use close at hand.

THE KITCHEN IS THE HEART OF THE HOME. EVERYTHING HAPPENS THERE

The kitchen is a living room that you can work in, but everyone lives and cooks differently, so lay it out for the way you do things. Put the oven where you want it, not where it's supposed to go. Warming drawers are perfect for some, and ice machines for others. A grill's great, but not if you don't use it. Think about an extra fridge or a lower cabinet for the kids so they don't have to climb up to get things. Dual dishwashers are the best, because you never have to unload them.

Kitchens are people
magnets, so make yours
comfortable and beautiful.
If the island has a counter
with stools, friends can hang
out while you're cooking.

FUNCTION AND STYLE GO HAND IN HAND, EVEN IN THE HARDWORKING ROOMS

There's no reason not to make your laundry and powder room just as fun and inviting as the rest of your house. You certainly spend enough time in them. The powder room in this loft doubles as the guest bath, so in addition to a shower and tub, I've added lots of touches to dress it up, like the artwork, the accessories, the ottoman, and, yes, a ladder for a towel rack. Add a few candles when company comes, and what could be more gracious?

Why not make your laundry room feel like part of the house? Put in a phone and artwork. All sorts of chic products are available—and washers and dryers have never looked so good.

The powder room also doubles as the guest bath, so I've made it a space that's dual purpose and stylish. A ladder for a towel rack is inviting and unexpected.

The slate counter, frameless glass doors, and tub definitely say today. The wood-seated toilet and subway tiles recall the loft's original period. The cork flooring is eco-friendly.

Case Study #2 BEDSIDE MANNERS

A bedroom is a home's most personal space, but it's also a place for more than just sleeping. It should be comfortable and inviting—a serene, multifunctional retreat for any time of the day and night.

BEFORE

Design really can make dreams come true. Take Sherri Burmester, a breast cancer survivor and mother of two in suburban St. George, Utah. Sherri and her husband devote everything to the kids, so decor was on the back burner, especially in the master suite. As she wrote in her entry to the Serta Counting Sheep for the Cure Bedroom Makeover program with Susan G. Komen: "My nightstands are plastic; we have no dresser drawers; and my comforter, well, it's twelve years old."

I wanted her bedroom to pamper and comfort her, and to function in more ways than one. She had an 18-by-13-foot space with lots of pluses: a walk-in closet, big bay window, cathedral ceiling, lots of light, and an attached bath with a soaking tub and a separate shower. Her furniture was in the right place, but the stuff itself was wrong, the windows were bare, and the lighting wasn't great. There was also an unsightly jog on one wall, which made the room's architecture feel off-kilter.

With furnishings and curtains from JCPenney, I've created distinct working, relaxing, and dining areas. A chic Karastan carpet installed by Salt Lake City's Custom Floors Company anchors the room. Striped walls in Benjamin Moore's Fernwood Green and Sandlot Gray add zip.

The space was great, but the room didn't look or feel good. Now it's a multifunctional retreat with areas for family activities, dining, work, and reading. Comfortable chairs and an ottoman encourage Sherri to put her feet up, and a proper desk doubles as a crafts and dining table. Everyone can gather around the entertainment center for a movie.

Sherri can use the desk for in-room dining (a hotel luxury at home) in the afternoon when she needs to reboot, or for a quiet, intimate dinner with her husband.

Family comes first with photos on the wall. Sherri's one really good piece of furniture, the chest at the foot of bed, is a passed-down heirloom.

The upholstered wing chairs and the ottoman create a place to relax alone or watch a movie with the family.

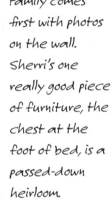

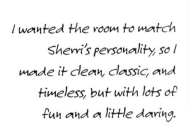

I wanted the room to match Sherri's personality, so I made it clean, classic, and timeless, but with lots of fun and a little daring.

TALKING POINTS

Design is a dialogue. It's that chat we have with ourselves, our friends, and our families, the way we figure out how to decide matters of style or of the heart. But it's also specifically the language of objects, how they relate to us and to each other, and the way we use what we live with to express who we are. At home, comfort comes first. But every room should be a beautiful backdrop for the life you and your family live. Whether you're buying antiques or new furnishings, you can find lots of options and some smart, stylish, personal, unique, and interesting pieces. Design that's authentic and that fits your lifestyle is a gift. The real luxury is to have an interesting life.

I counterbalanced this jutting jog on the wall with a curvaceous arched bracket.

Sherri's dream was an upholstered headboard and bedside tables with storage; I wanted the bed to be yummy, too.

Colors and patterns should coordinate, not match. The chocolate brown wool rug anchors the room, and the dhurrie establishes the tones of the autumnal palette.

Case Study #3 A WINNING PAIR

Dress My Nest is all about creating interiors that reflect your personality and translating it into individualized decor. But what happens if someone else suddenly moves in? For this just-hitched celeb couple, merging two disparate styles meant double the fabulousness.

When *E! News* anchor Giuliana DePandi purchased her LA condo, she was living the fast-forward life of a glam go-getter. With a crammed work and social schedule, she wanted a bachelorette pad that was low-maintenance, sleek, and chic. But she ended up with bare floors, an off-putting white sofa, and a dining table so deeply grooved it toppled drinking glasses. Then the Italian native married Bill Rancic, a successful entrepreneur and the first winner of *The Apprentice*. After he moved in, it quickly became clear that Giuliana's single-gal minimalism—"the place resembled a Ferrari showroom," recalls Bill—needed some couple-friendly coziness. To help the newlywed lovebirds, I asked them to choose favorite wardrobe and personal items to guide the decorating process. Their picks, including Giuliana's blinged-out jeans with crystal skulls and a sculptural Italian woman-of-the-year award, plus Bill's tailored polo shirt and engagement photos, influenced the design's haute-meets-homey aesthetic. Switching the palette from a harsh brown and white to a soothing grayish-green, and wallpapering with overscale botanicals, instantly softened the look. A beckoning, 12-foot-long sectional sofa and a round dining table added even more warmth. "The penthouse is so comfy now, we love coming home at the end of the day," says Giuliana.

BEFORE

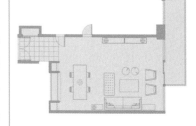

Me with telegenic twosome Giuliana and Bill Rancic, *left.* Pre-makeover, the living/ dining area of Giuliana's condo, *above,* was overpowered by a wall, lacquered in high-gloss chocolate brown, which made the space seem cold and cavernous. Pale bamboo floors without carpeting and an impractical white sofa— "guests were afraid to sit on it," Giuliana admits—were only exacerbating the problems.

Throw pillows with glinting, shimmery patterns introduce a fashion-y moment, and reference Giuliana's sassy, sexy wardrobe.

A sophisticated silver lamp helps integrate a history-steeped antique Chinese cabinet, a gift from Giuliana's sister, into the modern decor.

A generously proportioned white wooden mirror and compact Lucite table create insta-drama in the foyer, and hint at the juxtapositions to come.

Giuliana's original coffee table was still serviceable and stylish. All it needed: a deep-pile wool rug underneath to play down the hard edges.

Both the capiz-shell chandelier and octopus triptych remind the ocean-loving couple of their fairy-tale wedding in Capri.

Giuliana perches on a velvet-upholstered ottoman that offers flexible seating during the couple's frequent fêtes.

TRICKED-OUT WALLS CAN BE AS EYE-CATCHING AS ARTWORK

Like a lot of new construction, the condo had boxy dimensions and lacked architectural detail. To fake depth and keep the eye roving, I went all-out with wall treatments. A textural, subtly striped grasscloth, *right*, was cut into squares and hung in alternating directions, so the light catches each piece differently. As an accent, I covered the largest wall, *above*, with bold botanicals inspired by the silver leaves on Giuliana's Italian woman-of-the-year award. The hue links the area to the kitchen's charcoal gray cabinetry, and the blown-up print is like a chic chick's take on grandma's old-fashioned wallpaper.

Case Study #4 GREEN HOUSE EFFECT

This pioneering, eco-responsible Manhattan condo is proof that saving the planet doesn't mean sacrificing a sense of style. It's chic, livable, and loaded with smart solutions for reducing your own home's environmental impact while upping its wow factor.

Many people still think that in design, green has to be lean: less color, less texture, less variety, less fun, less personality. But I don't believe it. Green design is design that's appropriate, stylish, and inviting, and creates a friendly environment that's environmentally friendly in every way. Like the interior of this 2,500-square-foot model apartment in Riverhouse, the 264-unit condominium in New York's Battery Park City that's earned the top eco-responsible rating from the U.S. Green Building Council.

I thought the three-bedroom apartment (now two, with a den/home office) would be perfect for a pair of empty nesters moving downtown from the Upper East Side. You know these people: they're well-traveled, sophisticated, and curious, and they love to entertain family and friends. To fit the space to that couple, I fiddled a bit with the floor plan. Then I filled the interior with entirely sustainable or recycled materials, tribal art objects, patterned textiles, antiques, vintage pieces, new pieces made with all-green or repurposed materials, and low-VOC (that's volatile organic compounds) paints, finishes, and adhesives.

This building has all the latest stuff when it comes to sustainability, energy efficiency, indoor air quality, and water-saving features. It's also got amenities like photovoltaic cells that generate solar power and ultraviolet lights that kill bacteria in the pool. It's also full of beautiful, eco-friendly materials. Trust me, it was an honor and an inspiration to have an opportunity to show off its incredible possibilities.

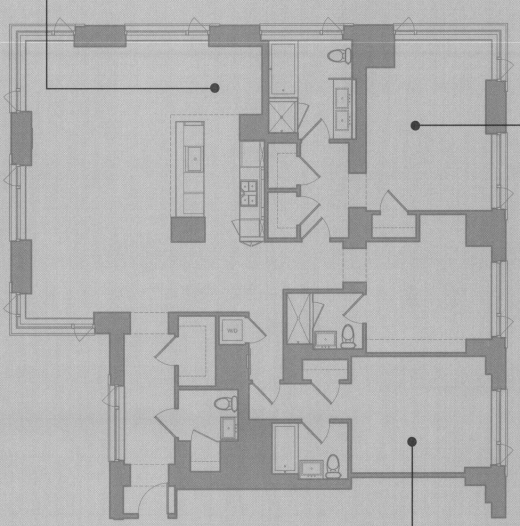

The dining room area flows organically into the living room and the kitchen. I built in the banquette (who doesn't love a window seat?) for balance. The vintage étagère in the wall niche adds extra storage for books.

Thanks to its corner location, the master bedroom (en suite with the bath) is flooded with natural light and has phenomenal views in two directions.

For privacy, the guest bedroom has an attached bath, seating, and storage, plus a beautifully dressed bed. It's a self-sufficient haven—and as comfortable a home away from home as any visitor could wish.

THE ARCHITECTURE OF A SPACE HAS EVERYTHING TO DO WITH HOW YOU FEEL IN IT

Some spaces just make you feel better than others, even if you can't say why. But architecture matters: usually those good vibes come from well-modulated volumes, an organic floor plan, and lots of natural light. This apartment had all those things. But it needed a little bit of rhythm, especially at the entrance. So I built in a couple of wood archways (painted white) to frame a vestibule and the entry to the main living area. The only other significant structural changes I introduced were in the den/home office (formerly a bedroom): replacing the doorway with the white wood archway connected it to the rest of the public spaces, and pulling out a closet created a work space.

The dining area balances the living area. And with plenty of pull-up seating and the banquette, it suits a sit-down dinner for eight or a cozy meal for two.

Symmetry can bring stability, so I've framed the living room sofa with pairs of tables and chairs.

Turn an oversized hallway into an efficient multitasking space. This bar between the living and sleeping areas introduces much-needed storage and a spot for extra chairs.

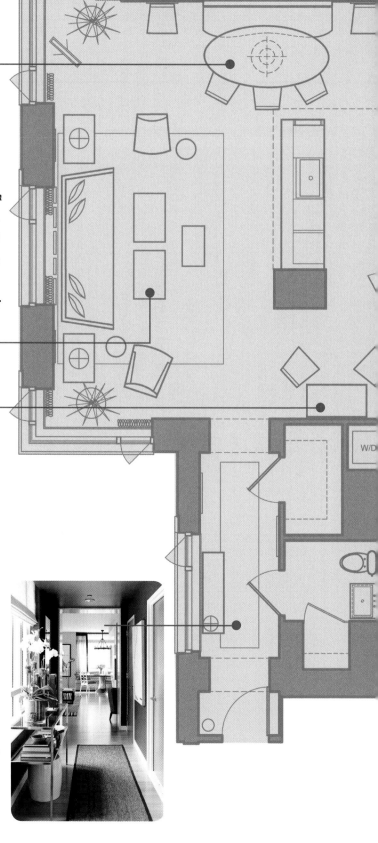

Every entry should have a little drama. To make this one intimate and sexy, I used a saturated-red woven grasscloth and painted the doors and ceilings charcoal.

Focal walls, like the one behind the four-poster, anchor a room. This eco wallpaper with metallic ink does wonderful things to light.

The L-shaped sofa I designed for the den is constructed of natural, hypoallergenic latex foam.

Now's the time to discover many shades of green: I made the bed using all eco-friendly materials. The chest of drawers is crafted of recycled picture frames.

There's green, greener, and tree hugger. Why not try all three together? That's what I did in the living room. For a wow moment and to disguise a vertical window casing, I had artist Bryan Nash Gill create a focal point in the window from a downed Connecticut sycamore.

THERE ARE COUNTLESS WAYS TO GO GREEN, SO LET'S START COUNTING

Green design should be a no-brainer. When it is, you won't see it (like here, I hope). These floors are bamboo (nothing grows faster); for equally minimal environmental impact, try revival flooring made from reclaimed soft- and hardwood. For furnishings and millwork, opt for woods certified by the Forest Stewardship Council (FSC). Organic foams are available, and so are eco-smart glues, adhesives, and finishes, low-VOC paints, and vegetable-dyed, natural-fiber fabrics and rugs. Furnishings that are vintage, antique, repurposed, or custom-designed with eco-friendly materials reduce environmental stress. I made the dining-table top of PaperStone and the base of recycled zinc. And that's just the beginning.

An oversized Roberto Dutesco photograph depicting the untamed horses on Canada's Sable Island brings nature-themed drama to the space.

When you're creating a room within a room, try working from the ground up. The rug that defines the living room is pieced together from vintage kilim runners and cut-up felt the color of the entry hall ceiling.

Green design comes in all shades, most of them peachy (keen, that is). So when you're going green or upping your existing eco-style quotient, think about your makeover in terms of two classic hues: hunter and sage. That's what I do, because designers are hunters after smart solutions and wise choices—like sustainable, reclaimed, and certified materials.

You really can create a high-impact, environmentally friendly space the same way you would any other. All you have to do is concentrate on the three *Rs*: recycle, reuse, reduce. Vintage or antique furnishings and accessories give every room a great shout-out of personality (yours).

There's an amazing assortment of green products now available, and more on the way every day. Try beeswax or soy candles and fabrics made of organic fibers (silk, wool, cotton, linen, hemp, and bamboo, a miracle fiber, honestly). Check out organic sponges and organic rubber foams for pillows and upholstery. And always try water-based finishes and adhesives and low-VOC paints first. You can also look for sustainable woods certified by the FSC and switch to low-watt fluorescent bulbs. Green even applies to the art: here I've opted for mostly oil- or ink-based pieces and sculpture from natural roots and fibers. More and more companies are making things of recycled metals, glass, ceramics, and even plastics. Plus there are healthy, toxin-free cleaning products for your home and laundry (if you don't like the way they're packaged, you can find all sorts of sexy reusable containers for them).

One other simple way to start your green evolution is to use your thumb and put a tree, or at least a potted plant, in every room. Growing things give every space a visible lift—and your heart, too.

EASY WAYS TO MAKE PEACE WITH GREEN

Yes, Riverhouse was conceived from the ground up as an environmentally sensitive project. But to start greening your home, you don't have to demolish your place completely (think of the landfill) only to rebuild it again. There are plenty of small ways to give yourself a meaningful eco makeover right away. So try being a conscious consumer: stick with products that are organic, biodegradable, sustainable, renewable, repurposed—and, of course, good-looking.

I've put organic references everywhere, from the puzzle-tree sculpture to the ceramic side tables to the bird sculptures roosting on the side tables.

This fab glass lamp is one of a pair I made by repurposing antique wine bottles (and they're green). I like using glass lamps because they don't hog the visual space.

When it comes to green design, there's a lot to learn—and a lot to love.

You can do a lot with a lampshade. I've used a natural texture here, trimmed with woven chain detail (yes, circles and ovals are everywhere).

A globe-trotter's interior can and should have its visually quiet moments, like the tranquil tableau of dark-glazed, matte-finished ceramics atop a silver tray on my custom-made low-VOC lacquered white coffee tables.

DESIGN'S A BALANCING ACT, AND EVERY ROOM HAS ITS OWN EQUILIBRIUM

There's no real formula or recipe to design, just careful calculation and a good sense of proportion. Balance (unlike symmetry) tends to lie under the radar. It's all about opposites and complements: weight and weightlessness, texture and pattern, color and light, matte and shiny, thick and thin, the curved and the straight, the new and the old. Here, layers of natural materials like woods, metals, glass, and ceramics create visual equilibrium.

The telescope is a great vintage piece, and I thought it was a fun addition because the views from this apartment are amazing—and every urbanite is a bit of a peeping Thom.

MAKING A PROPER ENTRANCE

Inviting design puts you in the mood for what's to come. Think about it this way: your home is your sanctuary, so why not use the decor to bliss you out as soon as you walk in the front door? If you pare down your entryway to the essentials, you can still create anticipation of what's to come. Keep it simple: a window shade that filters light but obscures an uninteresting view, and somewhere elegant to put favorite objects (and mail and keys). Look for honest forms, pieces that show pride in craftsmanship and don't try to be something they're not.

For effortless decor that's timeless and fresh, look for ways to stow (or at least organize) stuff. Every entry should have a table just for that purpose.

Quirky, elegant vintage pieces, like this floor lamp made of plumbing parts and a chandelier constructed of jet-engine pieces, can add tons of personality.

Most designers love chairs. You should, too. They are form and function combined and expressed with infinite variety. Every room needs more than one kind of seating, especially seating that adapts easily to different uses.

You know how to change things up in your wardrobe, so think about your interior palette the same way.

BUILD A BASIC PALETTE WITH A MIX OF NATURAL NEUTRALS

From the floor to the walls to the windows, upholstery, and bedding, I used plenty of color, pattern, and texture—with not a synthetic among them. First, let's talk fibers: wool, silk, cotton, linen, wood pulp (yup, that's what paper's made of), bamboo, kapok. There's bold color from vegetable dyes, too: the same strong, earthy shades of red, blue, mustard, and cocoa travel through the house from seating and eco–wall coverings to the pieced-together items made of repurposed materials (like a patchwork rug of felt and kilims).

To tie the den/home office to the rest of the house, I used elements from the entry: the grasscloth, the charcoal paint (on the desk wall and behind the books), and the white-painted woodwork.

REST EASY IN A BOUDOIR THAT PLAYS UP THE GORGEOUSNESS OF GREEN DESIGN

High style goes low impact in the eco-modern master bedroom, which showcases innovative, chemical-free materials. The dramatic focal point of the space is the Asian-inspired, four-poster bed, *opposite*. Constructed of plantation-grown and recycled woods and layered with supersoft organic cotton sheets and shams, it's simultaneously sleek and sophisticated, and its angularity echoes the geometric precision of the organic-wool carpet. To help all those straight lines, I opted for an unusual circular piece of antique tribal artwork that's as eye-catching as it is exotic. Originally used as currency in Papua New Guinea, it's crafted from a single, continuous thread of nasa shells. Also amping up the earth-friendly factor: a lamp of repurposed ship's chain and a pair of round night tables I designed using orange linen sealed with water-based lacquer.

Contrast is how we see, and it's one of the ways we energize all our senses—and our spaces. It's also a basic principle of design and is why I've partnered the rattan pouf with the vintage glass-and-chrome desk.

A pair of his-and-hers shoe towers, built from sustainably harvested wood and topped with antique stone finials, stylishly organize footwear.

When it's time to replace it, swap your current mattress for a sleep system with more breathable, hypoallergenic eco materials. This mattress is soy and bamboo, with a kapok-filled throw pillow and a bamboo-knitted throw so soft it feels like cashmere.

References to nature can liven up an urban interior and add more layers of eco-friendliness.

TREAT VISITORS TO LUXE TOUCHES AND SUMPTUOUS SERENITY

Where better than a guest bedroom to show your appreciation of the understated and the elegant? Use your hard-won editing skills to create a space that welcomes with a wonderful hush. Ornamental flourishes can adorn rather than disrupt. And there are plenty of ways to layer on muted, toned-down decorative touches, like using the highest thread count cotton sheets you can afford and a beautiful hand-finished coverlet (or a great-looking imposter).

There's nothing greener than something growing, which is why I've added plenty of trees and plants.

In every room, I used good-for-the earth, pure paper wallpaper rather than the chemical-laden vinyl varieties. This metallic stunner adds texture and dimension and is so striking there's no need for additional artwork in the guest bedroom.

Talk about repurposed: I crafted the bedside tables from old sewing machine stands topped by reused stone. The lamp base is unglazed ceramic.

Case Study #5 FAMILY AFFAIR

Say hello to the Ethridge clan of Walpole, Massachusetts, the winners of my great room makeover contest. Their once–lackluster space went from drab to fab thanks to friendly furnishings, unifying hues and patterns, and meaningful touches that reflect each member's interests and personality.

BEFORE

Deena Ethridge's winning essay was a design SOS—with good reason. The Ethridge's proverbial "great room"—a two-story space with cathedral ceilings, skylights, hardwood floors, wall-mounted flat-screen TV, and cultured-rock fireplace—was such an eyesore that Deena and husband Reggie asked guests to keep their eyes wide shut. The five younger Ethridges had taken the space over, even with a playroom in the basement. But the Toys 'R' Us decor wasn't the only problem. The family furniture was stained, mismatched, and badly arranged, the recessed lighting inadequate, the wall color unpleasant, the curtains nonexistent, and a giant wood-and-brass ceiling fan dominated the air space.

A great room like this can be daunting. But if you choose pieces that suit the architecture, with classic shapes, textures, and patterns, you'll be on your way to creating a room that's for grown-ups and kids alike. Thanks to Ethan Allen's amazing selection, quality, and generosity, that's what I did here. These stylish made-to-last furnishings, fabrics, and accessories suit the Ethridges' lifestyle—and like them, they're fresh, classic, and fun, too.

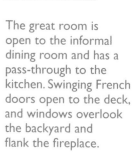

The great room is open to the informal dining room and has a pass-through to the kitchen. Swinging French doors open to the deck, and windows overlook the backyard and flank the fireplace.

The Ethridges didn't really need curtains for privacy, but these golden sheers with crewelwork give the room a beautiful finished look.

Simple finishes, clean lines, and crisp, modern style always look timeless. To integrate the TV into the room, I hung artwork above and below it.

Patterns add personality, but sometimes they do more. The ikat on the wing chairs refers to exotic locales where the Ethridges have gone on their travels.

When you walk into a room, you want to see an attractive elevation. The console behind the sofa back makes for an eye-catching first impression.

A two-story room gives you a great height advantage, so make the most of it.

Area rugs create rooms within rooms. This one's a strié with four colors that exactly match the tiles. So much fresher and younger than an oriental imposter, don't you think?

WHEN YOU'VE GOT IT, FLAUNT IT

If you have generous volume, use it. Choose and arrange your furnishings to anchor the space and to establish a comfortable visual hierarchy. The L-shaped sectional in a chevron-textured camel upholstery and comfortable club chairs in a chocolate-and-beige windowpane fabric (it reminds me of an exaggerated suit plaid) are the framework for the large seating area. The ikat-covered wing chairs and watermelon-covered ottoman create an intimate area by the fire and can join the conversational circle when more seating's needed. Sofas, chairs, lamps, bookcase, and artwork staggered at various heights move the eye up and down the walls.

DESIGN THAT'S ALL IN THE FAMILY

Meaningful mementos, like the mantel that Reggie built from tiles Deena's parents brought from Morocco, are great design springboards, and the room's color palette comes directly from the tiles. Since the Ethridges are enthusiastic travelers, I used books, silver-framed photos, and knickknacks from the family trips to give the space their sense of adventure. Maps, etchings of New York, Paris, and Venice, and framed fabrics from visits to Africa enhance the far-flung feeling. The materials, though, are classic New England: ebonized woods, forged metal lighting, steel accents, bronze, and glass. Rattan tables lighten things up. This is the Ethridge family room, and I wanted it to tell the Ethridge family story. You should do the same in yours.

Originally the mantel was white, but I painted it black to frame the Moroccan tiles that provided the room's color palette (neutrals and complementary shades, like the navy blue on the walls).

Bring It Home

This is just a sampling of my favorite go-to vendors and businesses. For a complete list, and tons more exclusive insider info, use the password on the back flap and log on to www.ThomFiliciaStyle.com. See you there!

FURNITURE AND ACCESSORIES

Aero
www.AeroStudios.com

Andrew Martin
www.AndrewMartin.co.uk

Angela Horton
www.AngelaHorton.com

Anthropologie
www.Anthropologie.com

B&B Italia
www.BeBitalia.it

Baker
www.KohlerInteriors.com

BDDW
www.BDDW.com

Bed Bath & Beyond
www.BedBathand
Beyond.com

Bergdorf-Goodman
www.Bergdorf
Goodman.com

Blackman Cruz
www.BlackmanCruz.com

British Khaki
www.BritishKhaki.com

**Calypso Home—
Christiane Celle**
www.Calypso-Celle.com

Cappellini
www.Cappellini.it

Carl Chaffee
www.CarlChaffee.com

Conran Shop
www.Conran.com

The Container Store
www.ContainerStore.com

Crate & Barrel
www.CrateandBarrel.com

Dennis Miller Associates
www.DennisMiller.com

Design Within Reach
www.DWR.com

Desiron
www.Desiron.com

Donzella
www.Donzella.com

Downtown
www.Downtown20.net

Dunbar
www.collectDunbar.com

Environment Furniture
www.Environment-
Furniture.com

Espasso
www.Espasso.com

George Smith
www.GeorgeSmith.com

Gorilla
www.GorillaFurniture.com

Grace Home Furnishings
www.GraceHome
Furnishings.com

H.D. Buttercup
www.HDButtercup.com

Hinson Lighting
www.HinsonLighting.com

Holly Hunt
www.HollyHunt.com

IKEA
www.Ikea.com

Intérieurs
www.Interieurs.com

JCPenney
www.JCPenney.com

Jerry Pair
www.JerryPair.com

John Derian Company
www.JohnDerian.com

John Houshmand
www.JohnHoushmand.com

Just Scandinavian
www.JustScandinavian.com

Karkula
www.Karkula.com

Knoll
www.Knoll.com

Kreiss
www.Kreiss.com

McGuire
www.KohlerInteriors.com

Mecox Gardens
www.MecoxGardens.com

Michael C. Fina
www.MichaelCFina.com

Ochre
www.Ochre.net

Oly Studios
www.Olystudio.com

Palecek
www.Palecek.com

Pearl River
www.PearlRiver.com

Pierce Martin
www.PierceMartin.com

Pottery Barn
www.PotteryBarn.com

Pottery Barn Kids
www.PotteryBarnKids.com

Pottery Barn Teen
www.PBTeen.com

Qcollection
www.Qcollection.com

Ralph Pucci International
www.RalphPucci.net

Red Envelope
www.RedEnvelope.com

Restoration Hardware
www.Restoration
Hardware.com

Richomme
www.RichommeInc.com

Roman Thomas
www.RomanThomas.com

Room and Board
www.RoomandBoard.com

Roost
www.Roostco.com

Sutherland Teak
www.SutherlandTeak.com

Takashimaya New York
www.NY-Takashimaya.com

Tenango
www.TenangoInc.com

Tribbles Home & Garden
www.TribblesHomeand
Garden.com

Tucker Robbins
www.TuckerRobbins.com

Tui Pranich
www.TuiPranich.com

Twentieth
www.Twentieth.net

Urban Outfitters
www.UrbanOutfitters.com

Vanguard Furniture
www.VanguardFurniture.com

Viesso
www.Viesso.com

West Elm
www.WestElm.com

Williams-Sonoma
www.Williams-Sonoma.com

Z Gallerie
www.ZGallerie.com

LINENS; FABRICS; WALL, WINDOW, FLOOR COVERINGS; AND TRIMS

Aleman Moore
www.AlemanMoore.com

Amadi Carpets
www.AmadiCarpets.com

AM Collections
www.AMCollections.com

Amenity
www.AmenityHome.com

Astek Wallcoverings
www.AstekWallcovering.com

B. Berger
www.BBerger.com

Beauvais
www.BeauvaisCarpets.com

Bergamo Fabrics
www.BergamoFabrics.com

Bobby Berk Home
www.BobbyBerkHome.com

Conrad Shades
www.ConradShades.com

Cowtan & Tout
www.Cowtan.com

DeLany & Long Ltd.
www.DelanyandLong.com

Donghia
www.Donghia.com

Double Knot
www.Double-Knot.com

Dwell Studio
www.DwellStudio.com

Edelman Leather
www.EdelmanLeather.com

Elizabeth Dow
www.ElizabethDow.com

F.J. Hakimian
www.FJHakimian.com

Flor
www.Flor.com

Holland & Sherry, Inc.
www.HollandandSherry.com

Innovations in Wallcoverings Inc.
www.InnovationsUSA.com

John Robshaw
www.JohnRobshaw.com

Karastan
www.Karastan.com

Kravet
www.Kravet.com

Lee Jofa
www.LeeJofa.com

Lulu DK
www.LuluDK.com

Maharam
www.Maharam.com

MDC Wallcoverings
www.Muraspecna.com

Merida Meridian, Inc.
www.MeridaMeridian.com

Odegard
www.OdegardInc.com

Osborne & Little
www.OsborneandLittle.com

Paul H. Lee Carpets and Rugs LLC
(203) 329-8683

Phillip Jeffries Ltd.
www.PhillipJeffries.com

Pollack
www.PollackAssociates.com

Sacco Carpet
www.SaccoCarpet.com

Safavieh
www.Safavieh.com

Samuel & Sons
www.SamuelandSons.com

Serta
www.Serta.com

Shaw Carpets
www.ShawFloors.com

Sister Parish Design, Inc.
www.SisterParishDesign.com

Stark Walcovering
www.StarkWallcovering.com

Town and Country Flooring
www.TNCFlooring.com

York Wallcovering
www.YorkWall.com

Zoffany
www.Zoffany.com

FINISHES, HARDWARE, FIXTURES, AND APPLIANCES

Amana
www.Amana.com

Blackman
www.Blackman.com

Boffi
www.Boffi.com

Circa Lighting
www.CircaLighting.com

E.R. Butler & Co.
www.ERButler.com

Gracious Home
www.GraciousHome.com

John Wigmore
www.JohnWigmore.com

Katonah
www.KatonahNY.com

Nanz
www.Nanz.com

New Ravenna
NewRavenna.com

Niche Modern
www.NicheModern.com

Regency Architectural Lighting
www.RegencyNY.com

Remains Lighting
www.Remains.com

Restoration Hardware
www.Restoration
Hardware.com

Rocky Mountain Hardware
www.RockyMountain
Hardware.com

Urban Archaeology
www.UrbanArchaeology.com

Urban Electric Co.
www.UrbanElectricCo.com

Vaughan
www.VaughanDesigns.com

Waterworks
www.waterworks.com

ART AND ANTIQUES

Acquisitions
www.AcquisitionsLA.com

Amy Perlin Antiques
www.AmyPerlinAntiques.com

Bill Lowe Gallery
www.LoweGallery.com

Bryan Nash Gill
www.BryanNashGill.com

Burden & Izett Ltd.
www.BurdenandIzett.net

Chista
www.Chista.net

De Vera
www.DeVeraObjects.com

Duane Modern
www.DuaneModern.com

Elizabeth Street Gallery
www.ElizabethStreet
Gallery.com

Eric Appel LLC
www.EricAppel.com

Far Eastern Antiques
www.FarEasternAntiques.com

Gottlieb Gallery
www.GottliebGallery.com

Gustavo Olivieri Antiques
www.GustavoOlivieri
Antiques.com

Where Credit Is Due

William Abranowicz: 49, 51, 119, 120, 122, 123, 146, 162
Antonis Achilleos: 22, 58, 66, 130, 134, 138, 142, 146, 150, 158, 180, 182, 208
Dale Berman: 192, 193, 194, 195
Jimmy Bishop: 188, 189, 190
Jeff Clark: 35, 36, 37, 38, 72, 84, 95, 159, 165
Paul Costello: 31, 32, 33, 40, 54, 55, 106, 116, 127, 135, 162
Jimmy Cohrssen: 84
Roger Davies: 86
Roberto Dutesco: 138
Laurie Frankel: 150
Getty Images: 125, 129, 133, 137, 141, 145, 149, 153, 157
François Halard: 108, 165
Brook Jacobs: 224
Thomas Loof: 48, 68, 75, 82, 101, 162, 165
Corvin Matei: 2, 3, 126, 130, 134, 138, 140, 142, 146, 158
Barbel Meibach: 47, 56, 72, 74, 78, 118, 121, 134, 154
Toshiaki Nozawa: 44, 88, 96, 102, 164
Eric Piasecki: 9, 41, 46, 64, 65, 67, 87, 88, 130, 131, 147, 162, 170, 171, 172, 174, 176, 177, 178, 179, 181, 183, 184, 186, 187, 198, 199, 200, 202, 204, 205, 206, 207, 209, 210, 211, 212, 213, 214, 215, 216, 217, 218, 219
Jason Schmidt: 50, 85, 104, 112, 113, 114, 117, 139, 151
Brad Stein: 42, 52, 59, 60, 61, 62, 69, 76, 77, 80, 126, 130, 134, 142, 154, 158, 162, 212
Thom Filicia Inc.: 30, 34, 107, 110, 111, 164
Jeffrey Thurnher: 11, 14
Jonny Valiant: 43, 70, 73, 81, 89, 92, 93, 94, 98, 99, 115, 154, 155

William Waldron: 17, 18, 20, 23, 24, 25, 26
Howard Wise: 45, 90, 91

Page 2: BACKDROP WALLCOVERING by Larsen. © 2007. All rights reserved.
Page 11, 14: Thom Filicia photos courtesy of Jeffrey Thurnher: The Style Network, © 2008 E! Entertainment Television, Inc. All rights reserved.
Page 13: Syracuse University Seal provided courtesy of Syracuse University. All rights reserved.
Page 15: Craig Blankenhorn/NBCU Photo Bank
Page 96: Artwork courtesy of Bob Moody
Page 107, 164: Courtesy of Thom Filicia Inc.
Page 126: Courtesy of Conrad Hand-woven Window Coverings
Page 134: Image of sconce courtesy of Intérieurs
Page 134: Image of candle courtesy of Molton Brown
Page 138: Image of tables courtesy of Knoll
Page 138, 150: Image of chairs courtesy of Cappellini
Page 142: Image of sconce courtesy of Urban Electric Co.
Page 143: TFI Sofa featured in a Larsen advertisement; photography by David Sawyer. © 2006 Cowtan and Tout, Inc. All rights reserved.
Page 150: Noble Stag design by Roost. Photo courtesy of Laurie Frankel Photography.
Page 106: Artwork courtesy of Alex Weinstein
Page 158: Kilim image courtesy of Double-Knot Rugs
Page 30, 31, 34, 35, 169, 170, 188, 189, 192, 194, 197, 198, 214, 215: Floor plans courtesy of Sarah Barrett and Wade Hui

stay tuned for more...

ATRIA BOOKS

A Division of Simon & Schuster, Inc.
1230 Avenue of the Americas
New York, NY 10020

First Atria Books hardcover edition October 2008

ATRIA BOOKS and colophon are trademarks of Simon & Schuster, Inc.

For information about special discounts for bulk purchases,
please contact Simon & Schuster Special Sales at
1-800-456-6798 or business@simonandschuster.com.

Designed by Doug Turshen with Stephen Turner

Manufactured in the United States of America

10 9 8 7 6 5 4 3 2 1

Library of Congress Cataloging-in-Publication Data

Filicia, Thom.
  Thom Filicia style : inspired ideas for creating rooms you'll love /
Thom Filicia.
     p. cm.
 1. Interior decoration. 2. Filicia, Thom. I. Title.

NK2115.F418 2008
747—dc22
                              2008027035
ISBN-13: 978-1-4165-7218-3
ISBN-10:   1-4165-7218-X